# kindness
(a user's guide)

*For everybody. And especially Andy Harrison, Edward Woolley,
Jane Giles and the Hanoush family. And our mums.*

A STUDIO PRESS BOOK

First published in the UK in 2021 by Studio Press,
an imprint of Bonnier Books UK,
The Plaza, 535 King's Road, London SW10 0SZ
Owned by Bonnier Books,
Sveavägen 56, Stockholm, Sweden

www.bonnierbooks.co.uk

1 3 5 7 9 10 8 6 4 2

ISBN 978-1-8007-8105-4

Written by Ali Catterall and Kitty Collins
Edited by Stephanie Milton
Designed by Nia Williams
Production by Emma Kidd

A CIP catalogue for this book is available from the British Library.
Printed and bound in Latvia

# kindness
(a user's guide)

# ali catterall & kitty collins

STUDIO
PRESS

# Introduction

First things first: the authors claim zero bragging rights to this concept. As evinced by our social media presence, and as some of our exes will doubtless tell you, we too have been, and will surely continue to be, absolute gits on occasion. Like you, we're just trying to figure it all out. Indeed, there's an argument for suggesting that anyone who elects themselves an ultimate arbiter of Kindness is almost certainly bound for a bit of a fall. As a wise man once said, you don't get to mark your own homework. In short, this isn't preening – it's *striving*.

Secondly, we are all too aware of the era in which this is being published. No book is written in a vacuum (except *An Inside History of the Vacuum Cleaner*) and this one's no exception. As we write, Britain has the highest coronavirus death rate on the planet and is suffering its biggest economic slump for 300 years. The worst president in the history of the United States, who stood on a platform of cruelty and racism, has just been acquitted from his second impeachment. (As an aside, can we agree never to elect former gameshow hosts as leaders ever again. Except perhaps the late Humphrey Lyttelton. Or RuPaul.)

Meanwhile, a pitiless, ideological Culture War, a nil-sum game stoked by offshore press barons and billionaires, covertly funded think tanks, attention-seeking contrarians and shame-deficit leaders, has pervaded almost every aspect of the discourse; acting as an effective smokescreen for some desperately urgent problems. The world is burning. To speak of Kindness right now feels frankly like an indulgence. In the words of a random YouTube comment, presumably left by a kindly time-traveller, "If you are reading this in 2021, you are a legend." To which we can only reply: yep. (And if you're reading this in the future, and things have become even *worse*, you have our profoundest sympathies.)

However, to paraphrase Oscar Wilde: though we may be in Hell, some of us are trying to snuff out the flames. It would be impossible to write a contemporary book on Kindness without referencing the global pandemic, during which millions of frontline workers have risked their lives to save others. Teachers, carers, postal workers, delivery drivers and retailers have provided vital services or pivoted to keep their communities going, during this bewildering, frightening, and utterly heartbreaking moment of Big History. Thousands of volunteers are training themselves up to help with the vaccination drive: that nurse helping to process your forms may have been an actor or Hollywood screenwriter in the Before Times. During a recent Super Bowl game, one of the team's defence lines was weakened, as a key player had returned to medicine to combat the virus. Dystopias have rarely been more selfless or benevolent. In truth, we could have written an entire book about Kindness in the time of Covid.

And amid tragedy upon tragedy, green shoots are poking through. Last year, Joe Biden won more votes than any other presidential candidate in US history after campaigning on a platform of healing division; the Design of the Year 2020 was a collection of bright pink see-saws allowing people to interact across the US-Mexico border; and by the time you read this, millions more around the globe will have received their lifesaving vaccines. The world is waking up.

This book contains 52 stories – a Kindness for every week of the year, although we'd probably recommend dipping into it at random as opposed to reading it all in one go. Too many salted caramels at once can be bad for the digestion. Please look upon these stories, quotes and tips as signposts or potential pathways. Kindness takes many forms. Within these pages are remarkable examples of humanity and acting for the greater good – all of them testament to the fact that where love isn't always possible, kindness always is.

It's in our nature, too. If philosophers such as Thomas Hobbes argued that humans were inherently selfish (calling to mind the satirist Tom Lehrer's remark that philosophers enjoy giving helpful advice to people who are happier than they are), recent psychological studies suggest a sense of morality or fairness has become a feature of the human brain as a result of evolution. It's just that we're not always aware of our own instinctive altruism.

However, this whole Kindness thing shouldn't be self-consciously performative, either. As we've discovered, some of the loudest voices wielding the hashtag #BeKind like an iron wand appear to be anything but. (Conversely, some of the grumpiest people are also among the kindest in our experience.) The mere act of referring to oneself as kind does not in itself bestow Kindness upon the wearer. Kindness is habitual; not a shrill self-designation or glass-tapped proclamation, but an ingrained behaviour, manifested through acts (unsung or otherwise), and made stronger through practice. Don't tell us – show us.

Some will argue, in these times, that Resistance is more important than Kindness, as if Kindness itself was not a type of resistance, or that Resistance couldn't possibly lead to tyranny on either side. If Resistance is certainly an immediate political priority, we also firmly believe in Kindness as a political act. To ransack media theorist Marshall McLuhan, maybe a good way of framing this is "Resistance as the Medium, Kindness as the Message".

While the authors are unapologetically on the left, Kindness is, or ought to be, beyond political or tribal affiliations. It should be beyond religion, too: the phrase "Do unto others as you would have them do unto you", also known as The Golden Rule, may recur across almost all the world's major faiths, from Zoroastrianism to Islam, but irrespective of religion, Kindness should ideally be at the heart of everything we are and everything we do.

It feels like a daunting task. But within the smallest icicle lies an ocean. Four of the kindest words you can say to someone right now are, "It's not just you." It's like an instant verbal hug. In three words? Try, "Are you okay?"

And Kindness, as they say, is catching. Obviously, the greater exposure we have to it, the better. And some people are better – or worse – at spreading it around. Right about now, it's clear to see we need all the infections we can get. Ideally, you might say, a pandemic. So, let us make a pact to try and open ourselves up to it – an ongoing, lifelong initiative we can experience both as receivers and givers. Even if just, as the Buddhist teacher Susan Piver suggests, for the sheer joy of doing so.

In a perfect world run by perfect leaders, this would simply be a matter of proximity. While technology has placed us, literally, in one another's pockets, it's a poor substitute for real human contact. Due to factors far beyond our control, and particularly at the time of writing, something as straightforward yet powerfully effective as a hug hasn't always been manageable. It's fair to say that never again will we take a simple handshake for granted. Yet always, there are opportunities. Any form of contact is an excellent place to start, even simply reaching out to one's neighbour to help, or listen. Unless we can embrace the concept of walking in one another's shoes for that proverbial mile, we are rather lost. Yet, in this too, empathy is noble but ineffectual unless followed up by compassion. Empathy could be considered a stepping-stone to compassion.

Kindness is free, readily available, instantly drawn at source. The key to unlocking the answer to the question "How to be kind" is beautifully, maddeningly, gloriously Zen. It is to truly understand that Kindness is attained by being kind – habitually, graciously and without expectation of reward. And then we might really start to rebuild a better and more compassionate world.

*Ali Catterall and Kitty Collins, 14 February 2021.*

. . . . . . . . . . . . . . . . . . . . . . . . . . . . . .

A small act is worth a million thoughts.

**Ai WeiWei**

# Love is like a bibliophile

She's been called everything from the Iron Butterfly to the Smoky Mountain Songbird and the Backwoods Barbie. But to millions of children around the world, she's known very simply as the Book Lady. An offshoot of her non-profit Dollywood Foundation, the Imagination Library was created in 1995 by Dolly Parton from a desire to help youngsters fall in love with reading – a luxury denied her dad, who was unable to read or write. And so the Queen of Nashville packs books off to kids up to the age of five, completely free of charge. As she told *CBS This Morning* in 2020, "I just felt like that if kids can learn to read early on, they're not afraid of it."

Initially launched in Tennessee, the mission blew like an early morning breeze across the US, then Canada, the UK, Australia and the Republic of Ireland; to date, over 135 million books have been hurtling their way through the postal systems. As for her latest nickname, she adores it. "That is one of the sweetest things ever in my whole career," she told CBS. "When the kids get their little books, they always say it's from the Book Lady. So I take pride in that. Whatever it takes to get them to love the books and to learn to read, I'm all about that." In April 2020, during the pandemic's first lockdown, the Queen of Country began a 10-week bedtime reading slot called Goodnight with Dolly, to comfort kids during a period of great anxiety. First out of the station was a live stream of Watty Piper's 1930 classic *The Little Engine that Could*. "I think it's pretty clear that now is the time to share a story and to share some love," she said.

Any more examples of Parton's wondrousness? How long have you got? To name a few: her Buddy Program aimed to reduce high school dropout rates during the early 90s through cash incentives; Dolly's My People Fund donated $1000 a month for six months to those who'd lost their homes in 2016's Great Smoky Mountains wildfires; while her annual Dolly Parton Scholarship awards $15,000 to high schoolers in Sevier County, Tennessee, to help them through college.

Dolly's true (coat of many) colours have been apparent for a long time. As Sarah Smarsh's Parton biography *She Come By It Natural* details, she's made a trajectory from being the butt of bosom-based punchlines to universally beloved icon status, strutting her stuff in a spotlight where women of a certain vintage have typically been invisible. This is the ultra-hard-working, proto-feminist who forbade Elvis to record 'I Will Always Love You' after his ruthless manager Colonel Tom Parker demanded 50% of the publishing royalties.

And then to top it all, in November 2020 it was reported that Dolly Parton had saved the entire planet. Parton, via her own Covid-19 research fund, had donated $1 m to Vanderbilt University in Nashville, Tennessee, who had been working rather more than 9 to 5 in their efforts to find a cure for coronavirus. Dolly had volunteered the sum after her doctor friend Naji Abumrad, who had once treated her after a car accident, told her all about "some exciting advancements" they were making. The result was the nearly 95% effective Moderna vaccine. (Cue instant choruses all round of "Vaccine... vaccine... vaccine... vacc-iiiiiiiiine..." to the tune of 'Jolene'.)

Her benevolence is beyond compare, with peroxide locks of bright blonde hair. And if the world is to have any kind of real-life superhero, the lady who bounced round the stage like a jumping bean at Glastonbury while honking Yakety Sax on a rhinestone-studded saxophone surely qualifies for that honour. What. A. Woman.

• • • • • • • • • • • • • • • • • • • • • • • • •

## If you see someone without a smile today, give 'em yours.

**Dolly Parton**
(Twitter post, 2019)

# True colours

In 2005, Spain became only the third country in the world to legalise same-sex marriage. Research in 2013 found a whopping 88% of the population said "Hola!" to their LGBTQ+ friends, making it one of the most unprejudiced places on Earth.

So it'd be natural to assume that, when it came to Pride celebrations, the fabulous rainbow emblem would be fluttering from every stiffened flagpole. In your dreams, girlfriend: thanks to a Spanish Supreme Court ruling, only the official flags of Spain, its regions, or the EU flag may be flown from council buildings. And while larger cities and towns openly flouted the law without repercussions, that wasn't the case for little Villanueva de Algaidas on the Costa del Sol.

In June 2020, an eight-metre long rainbow flag proudly flew from the town hall, showing solidarity for the LGBTQ+ community – something it had done to mark Pride Month since 2018. But after just 48 hours, three residents demanded its removal, citing a ruling issued in response to the use of Separatist flags – a ruling which was *in no way* intended to marginalise the LGBTQ+ community. Nevertheless, local officials had no choice but to order the flag be taken down.

Antonio Carlos Alcántara, a Torremolinos shopkeeper who had grown up in Villanueva de Algaidas, had a beautifully simple solution. "It bothered me that they had to pull down a flag that wasn't hurting or bothering anyone," he told the Guardian. Having pre-ordered hundreds of flags ahead of Pride (which was now cancelled due to Covid), he took to the town's Facebook page to offer them gratis to anyone who wished to wave one. Responses poured in: "The whole village wanted to put up a flag." Quicker than you can say "There's no place like home", this typical *pueblo blanco* (white town) was transformed, *Wizard of Oz*-style, into a riot of colour, as 500 flags billowed brightly from balconies and bars. Meanwhile, the council says that even if they're not allowed to fly the flag, they will *always* stand for tolerance, equality, open-mindedness and respect.

Kindness is to stand in the shoes of the outsider, the unfavoured, the 'stranger', and having stood in those shoes change the world, so it is better for them as well as you. Like different colours in the rainbow flag we exist side by side, different but equally important to the whole. Long before the flag came along we stood together in protest and in celebration, all of us so different yet so alike because we wanted the world to be fairer, and just and decent. Now we stand with those same values and the flag announces us.
Vive la différence!

**Lord Michael Cashman**
(co-founder of Stonewall, activist, actor, author)

## Kindness tip

Use your phone for its original intended purpose: speaking to people! Yep, actually pick up the phone and call a friend. Groundbreaking, right? And a bit scary. But feel the fear and do it anyway. Messages can be so impersonal, or they can get lost in translation or just ignored. All too often, a careless word or bust-up on social media between friends can also cause serious damage if left to fester – another reason to pick up the phone and talk things over properly. And if you're feeling particularly brave and fine of voice, sing a song down the phone. Encourage the recipient to do the same, making a whole chorus in the process. "Ring a friend/ sing a friend" has a certain ring to it.

Wherever there is a human being, there is an opportunity for a kindness.

(Attributed to Lucius Annaeus Seneca)

# Kindness tip

Next time you're entering a
supermarket and there's a
homeless person outside,
ask if you can get them
anything. Better still, ask them
what they actually need.
And even if you can't
contribute financially, perhaps
take the time to talk to them.

# It won't break the bank

Hurricane Katrina was one of the most ferocious hurricanes to ever hit the United States; the third deadliest, in fact, in US history. Reaching a windspeed of over 170 mph at its peak, followed by devastating floods, the 2005 Category 5 superstorm was responsible for over 1800 deaths, made millions more homeless in New Orleans, Louisiana, Mississippi and Alabama, and caused an estimated $100 bn of damage.

Infamously, it also exposed serious failings in the country's disaster response systems. While local, state and federal organisations were widely criticised for their handling of the tragedy, it ultimately led to the resignation of the director of the Federal Emergency Management Agency and did lasting damage to President George W Bush's reputation.

But one unlikely organisation did step up in the hour of need. Hancock Bank, a community bank founded in 1899, had itself been badly affected by the disaster. The head office in Gulfport, Mississippi was completely decimated, along with some 40 local branches. They had no electricity, no customer records, and most ATMs were out of service. Bank staff, too, had suffered their own personal tragedies and losses. But in the immediate aftermath, employees collected the literally filthy lucre from waterlogged banks, casinos and ATMs and quite literally laundered it. They washed and ironed banknotes, set up makeshift tables outside branches and did what they do best: they gave out money. To absolutely anybody who needed it. Whether they were an existing customer or not. With no computer records available, and many people not having access to ID or personal possessions, they operated a trust system, scribbling IOUs on scrap paper with just a name, address and social security number. In this way, the bank gave out around $42 m. As Hancock employee Gay Todd told CNN, "they looked after the community."

This act of faith was repaid in buckets. When almost all the money handed out was eventually returned, there was a shortfall of just $300,000. The bank's Chairman, George Schloegel, said, "Basically, people are honest and

want to do the right thing. And they'll stand by you if you stand by them."
George went on to become mayor of Gulfport in 2010 in a resounding victory, taking nearly 90% of the vote. There was another benefit, too: as communities started to rebuild, and life slowly returned to relative normality, grateful recipients put their money where their mouth was. By the following year deposits at the bank had increased by a whopping $1.5 bn. Kindness, it would seem, is good for business.

•  •  •  •  •  •  •  •  •  •  •  •  •  •  •  •  •  •  •  •  •  •  •  •

# The greatness of a community is most accurately measured by the compassionate actions of its members... a heart of grace and a soul generated by love.

**Coretta Scott King**
(Address at Georgia State University, 15 February 2000)

# A takeaway with a difference

*Strictly Come Dancing* winner Bill Bailey is one of Britain's most beloved comedians, not to mention a prominent animal rights campaigner, conservationist and author of a guide to British birds. Apropos of nothing, he's also the inspiration behind Underworld's mega techno-anthem 'Born Slippy'. One day in the 1990s the band's frontman Karl Hyde (who didn't know him), randomly passed Bill a fiver in the Ship pub in Wardour Street and asked him to "get a round in". We can only wonder what "lager, lager, lager"-style antics ensued.

Anyway. Some years ago, Bailey was visiting a restaurant in Beijing, the sort of place where diners choose their dishes from in-house cages and water tanks. And among the cages, he was shocked to spot a bird he recognised instantly: a live Eurasian eagle-owl – the largest owl species in the world.

"I decided to liberate it," he recalled. "So I told the waiter I wanted to eat first, and then take the owl away for later." As the waiter carried the owl to the kitchen, Bailey managed to make him understand he wanted to take it away – alive.

"They wrapped the poor bird's wings and feet in Sellotape and stuck it in a box marked 'Suitable for microwave ovens'," said Bill, who hailed a taxi and drove it into a forest to release it. Then, he phoned a friend – an owl expert at London Zoo.

"Don't worry so much about the beak, but watch out for the talons," his friend warned. "They can crush." As Bill held the wings, the taxi driver clutched the talons with a pair of oven gloves Bill had borrowed from the restaurant.

"There is no Chinese phrase book that gives you the words 'You hold the owl's feet while I cut the Sellotape off with the nail scissors'," said Bill. "But somehow I made him understand, and we did release the owl and watch it fly off into the forest." As they say in Mandarin, 做得好比尔 (Well done, Bill!)

If I can stop one heart from breaking
I shall not live in vain
If I can ease one life the aching
Or cool one pain
Or help one fainting robin
Unto his nest again
I shall not live in vain.

**Emily Dickinson**
('If I Can Stop One Heart From Breaking', 1864)

## Kindness tip

Got any old blankets or towels lying around?
Donate them to your local animal shelter,
who will bite your hand off for them. It's good for
the environment, and for keeping our four-legged
friends warm and cosy, too. And if you can,
throw in some pet food for good measure.

# Those who can, teach

Dubbed 'The Nobel Prize of Teaching', the Global Teacher Prize was established to raise the status of the teaching profession. The glamorous ceremony attracts worldwide attention – not least because of the $1 m prize. The only condition is that you must stay in teaching for five years. After that, you're free to spend the money as you wish.

In 2018, the award was won by Andria Zafirakou, an Art and Textiles teacher from Alperton Community School in the London borough of Brent, who headed off some 30,000 nominations from 173 countries. The school is situated in one of the most ethnically diverse areas in the country: 130 languages are spoken there, and pupils come from some of the poorest families in Britain.

As part of the school leadership team, Andria redesigned the curriculum from scratch, making it more relevant to the children. She tailored each class to the pupils and created alternative timetables, allowing girls-only PE lessons so as not to offend conservative communities. She also learnt the basics of 35 languages, to better communicate with her charges. She'd often be seen patrolling outside the school, warding off threats of gang and drug-related violence. She was even known to mend pupil's uniforms. Time and again she went above the call of duty, earning the trust and respect of her pupils and their parents.

If that wasn't enough, Andria used her $1 m to set up an arts foundation, Artists in Residence. At a time when the arts are being elbowed out of the curriculum, the foundation brings artist residencies to schools across the UK. It gives students the chance to develop skills across a range of disciplines, affords an insight into a career in the arts and aids teachers' professional development. Commented Andria on her decision, "This is something I won because I'm a teacher, so it's right to give it back to the profession." A lesson for us all.

The more I think about it,
the more I feel that there's
nothing more genuinely
artistic than to love people.

**Vincent Van Gogh**
(From a letter dated 18 September 1888 to his brother Theo,
thanking him for his financial support)

## Kindness tip

Take the time to really listen to children, with genuine
interest. Yes, they can be incredibly annoying
sometimes. But they are still deserving of your
attention. Put yourself in their shoes, and remember
how frustrating it was to be ignored as a child.
And always, ALWAYS answer a toy phone if a child
demands it. Embrace your inner kid. They will love you
for it, and you'll have a lot of fun along the way.

When you do something nice for somebody, forget it immediately. When someone does something nice for you, never forget it.

(Attributed to Jim Haynes)

# Kindness Tip

If someone is doing a good job, tell them — whether it's someone who works for you, a colleague or someone you've come across in your day-to-day life. Better yet, tell their boss. Who knows, it might even lead to a pay rise or a promotion, but at the very least you are acknowledging a job well done, and that goes a long way.

# Greetings from St James' Park

It was one of the most fraught, bitter and divisive 12 months in modern British political history. The miners' strike of 1984-1985 tore communities apart, resulted in the deaths of six people and left a legacy of acrimony that survives to this day.

Three months after the strike collapsed, in June 1985, Bruce Springsteen came to Newcastle to play a pair of gigs at Newcastle United's stadium, as part of his Born in the USA tour. A big fan of local band The Animals, Springsteen possibly felt a spiritual connection to this part of the world. The band ran through a repertoire including 'The River', 'Hungry Heart' and 'Born to Run', and tears could be seen in the crowd's eyes during his heartfelt rendition of 'My Hometown'.

Alan Cummings, the Durham Miners' Association secretary who was 38 at the time, picks up the tale. "[Springsteen] must have been aware of the hardship miners' families were facing," he recalled for North East news service Chronicle Live in 2018. And The Boss showed he had the human touch; Bruce privately handed a $20,000 cheque, the equivalent of nearly £40,000 in today's money, to the North East area support group for Durham and Northumberland. "That [cheque] came at a time we were really struggling," says Cummings. The cash was shared round equally, to help feed families like Alan's, whose son was 14 at the time.

Springsteen, well known for his charitable drives and benefits, did this quietly and without fanfare (financing in the dark, indeed), but, as Alan says, "obviously, these things trickle out. It was a huge amount of money to put into the system. His extraordinary gesture of solidarity was of great help to families who'd struggled through the year-long strike – and was an uplifting boost to morale." Baby, he was born to fund.

I consider myself to
be a kindness punk...
I really view my career,
and even what I'm doing now,
as a rebellion against all the
things in the world that
I see to be unkind...
Kindness heals people.

**Lady Gaga**
(From an interview with Oprah Winfrey,
Elle magazine, November 2019)

# Going underground

Her astonishing but necessarily secretive actions were rewarded merely by a "heartfelt 'God bless you'" from those she saved, as the great abolitionist Frederick Douglass once wrote. Yet, 100 years after her death, Barack Obama would hail Harriet Tubman as an American hero.

Born into slavery circa 1820, on a plantation in Maryland, Tubman was sent to work from the age of six. She was subject to regular beatings – on one occasion she was lashed five times before breakfast. At the age of 13 she suffered a near-fatal head injury at the hands of a slave master, causing lifelong dizzy spells, headaches, seizures and narcolepsy.

In 1849, following the death of her slave owner and fearing for her future as a sickly, frail slave with little to no economic value, she decided to escape with two of her siblings. Although they subsequently had second thoughts, she made the treacherous 90-mile passage from the South to the Free State of Philadelphia in the North, and to freedom. The escape was aided by the so-called 'Underground Railroad', which was neither underground nor a railroad. Rather, it was a transport network dotted with safe havens or 'stations', providing food and shelter along the way. These were mostly manned by former slaves, Quakers and abolitionists, and at great personal risk; the penalty for being caught was prison at best, death by hanging at worst. "When I found I had crossed that line, I looked at my hands to see if I was the same person," Tubman said on reaching Pennsylvania. "There was such a glory over everything; the sun came like gold through the trees, and over the fields, and I felt like I was in Heaven."

When a newly liberated Tubman received reports her niece was going to be sold, along with her two small children, she helped organise their escape, before becoming a 'conductor' on the Underground Railroad. At this point, things were even more dangerous: 1850 saw the introduction of the Fugitive Slave Act, whereby slaves could be recaptured, even in so-called Free States, and returned to their owners. The only safe haven was Canada. And the outlaws had to find ever-more ingenious methods. Most escapes were orchestrated on a Saturday – as Sunday was a day of rest, the slaves wouldn't be missed, and newspaper reports of missing slaves wouldn't be published until Monday, giving them a head start. They also used a sophisticated code system to plot escapes. Since many slaves were illiterate, it is believed they often used spiritual songs such as 'Wade in the Water' and 'Swing Low, Sweet Chariot' to pass on secret messages.

Tubman formed her own network, making the trip some 19 times, and helping approximately 300 people escape, fiercely proud of never once losing a life. Fondly known as 'Moses' for leading her people to freedom, she became so (in)famous that at one point she had a whopping $40,000 bounty on her head. That's over $1.2 m in today's money. When the Civil War started in 1861, Tubman joined the Union Army, initially as a nurse, but eventually taking on more dangerous responsibilities. One of the raids she led resulted in over 700 slaves being liberated.

After the Civil War, Tubman settled in New York State. She kept an open-door policy and helped anyone in need, surviving largely on donations and selling home-grown produce. Though illiterate, she'd also do speaking tours for the women's suffrage movement, of which she was a prominent supporter. In 1896 she opened the Harriet Tubman Home for Aged and Indigent Colored People, before dying of pneumonia in March 1913.

As Frederick Douglass wrote to her, "I have had the applause of the crowd... while the most that you have done has been witnessed by a few trembling, scarred and foot-sore bondmen and women. The midnight sky and the silent stars have been the witnesses of your devotion to freedom and of your heroism."

# A thread of kindness

If walls could talk, Manchester's Free Trade Hall wouldn't shut up. This is the venue in which Benjamin Disraeli gave his One Nation speech. It's the place where Christabel Pankhurst and Annie Kenney were thrown out of a meeting, after heckling Winston Churchill, before Christabel spat in a policeman's face – an action widely cited as the first act of Suffragette militancy. It's the spot where Bob Dylan was branded "Judas!" by heckler Keith Butler for having the impudence to plug a Telecaster in. And it's where the Sex Pistols played a gig so influential it's said that if everybody who claimed they were in the audience was actually there, the place would have been roomier than the TARDIS from Doctor Who. And it was also here, in 1862, that starving textile workers helped alter the course of history in another nation altogether.

That year, the shockwaves of Abraham Lincoln's Civil War against the breakaway Southern slave states were being keenly felt across the Atlantic. The north of England's 2400 mills (dubbed the "workshop of the world") supplied the West with a great many of its garments, making factory owners rich and keeping some 440,000 workers from going hungry. However, the clothes that came out of those mills were mainly spun from raw cotton picked by American slaves. Some three-quarters of those Southern plantation harvests were bound for Lancashire's looms.

Sanctioning slave-picked cotton, Lincoln argued, would thwart the Southern confederates and help restore the Union. But the resulting naval blockade decimated the industry – and many unemployed workers rioted and rebelled. In Liverpool, a city grown rich on cotton, Confederate flags fluttered in the breeze beside the Mersey. Even the Manchester Guardian reckoned it was better for workers to return to their spindles. Others took the opposite view: "Working men, I say the South is your enemy," Chartist Ernest Jones pleaded. "Slave labour is direct aggression on the free labour of the world."

That New Year's Eve, during a noisy meeting at the Free Trade Hall, those same desperate Lancashire cotton workers motioned to keep supporting the blockade and abolish slavery – to effectively vote against their own interests. The following year, Lincoln sent them a letter, the words of which can be read at the base of his statue in Manchester's Lincoln Square:

"I cannot but regard your decisive utterances on the question as an instance of sublime Christian heroism which has not been surpassed in any age or in any country." Relief ships soon arrived from the US, bulging with emergency provisions. And then, two years later, in January 1865, the Thirteenth Amendment was passed and slavery was abolished in the United States.

· · · · · · · · · · · · · · · · · · · · · · · · · · · · · ·

# When I do good I feel good, when I do bad I feel bad, and that's my religion.

**Abraham Lincoln**
(Quoted in *Herndon's Lincoln*, 1888)

# Pretty decent

By 1977, the Sex Pistols, with their singalong ditties about cultural tourism, gullible record labels and youthful ennui, were considered public enemy number one. However, for certain communities in West Yorkshire facing a very cold and hungry Christmas, they were anything but.

On Christmas Day, the Four Horsemen of the Snotty Lips discreetly rode up to the Ivanhoe Club in Huddersfield to perform a benefit gig for an equally reviled group – the striking firemen from the Fire Brigade Union and their families. This was inevitably a hush-hush affair: with the besieged group banned even from Holiday Inns ("like Mary and Joseph," as *The Great Rock 'n' Roll Swindle* director Julien Temple observed). The council would have gone completely tonto had they known.

First up was a children's matinee. "Johnny Rotten came out in a straw hat and they had a cake with Sex Pistols written on it, the size of a car bonnet," young Jez Scott recalled years later for the Guardian. "He started cutting it up but it soon degenerated into a food fight... it was fantastic." Covered in cake, the band tore through the likes of 'Anarchy in the UK', 'God Save the Queen' and 'Bodies' (apparently they toned the language down for that one, though lead singer John Lydon, ever the contrarian, denies this), as children pogoed and howled along. Meanwhile, Lydon, like some stick-thin Santa, handed out badges, t-shirts and skateboards for the kids, and ill-fated bassist Sid Vicious joined the teenagers on the dancefloor to the strains of Boney M's 'Daddy Cool' and Baccara's 'Yes Sir, I Can Boogie'.

It was the final gig they'd play in England until nearly 20 years later. Immediately before them lay a disastrous US tour and a murder rap. But that night, the big kids played to their most appreciative audience ever. "To most people they were monsters in the news," said Temple. "But seeing them playing to seven- and eight-year-olds is beautiful. They were a radical band, but there was a lot more heart to that group than people know."

In fact, Punk Rock means exemplary manners to your fellow human beings.

**Joe Strummer**
(From an interview in CD Now magazine, 1999)

# Rewriting the story

We all do things we regret. Some turn themselves into living signposts of hate, literally branded advertisements for cruelty. Fortunately, for those who want to change, help is at hand.

Tattoo-removal is usually a painful, pricey process. But in the wake of the Black Lives Matter movement, a tattoo parlour in Murray, Kentucky has been covering up hate tattoos free of charge. Jeremiah Swift and Ryun King of the Gallery X Art Collective ("a judgement free environment") dealt with 30 requests in the first week of posting their invitation on Facebook in 2020. They have since received thousands of enquiries and messages of goodwill from all over the world. "A lot of people, when they were younger, just didn't know any better and were left with mistakes on their bodies," Jeremiah told CNN. "We just want to make sure everybody has a chance to change." As the Gallery's Instagram post says, "Start your path to being the person you were meant to be."

Their first client was a woman sporting a Confederate flag, but who'd subsequently become an activist for racial equality. Another customer had a swastika on his chest – and had never been able to remove his shirt in front of children because of it. As swastikas are buried beneath garlands of roses or sunflowers, the relieved clients often relay their stories to the artists, bringing new meaning to the term art therapy. "As we're tattooing, we get to see the change in the person," King told the Huffington Post. "It's like they leave as a different person."

Over in Verona, in Italy, a street artist and restaurant worker called 'Cibo' (Italian for 'food') is doing similar good work, albeit on brick walls, effectively the skin of the city. In the country in which fascist movements first originated, and where a flirtation with neo-fascism is once more gaining a toehold, Cibo covers up racist graffiti with funky gastronomic murals – turning a swastika into a pumpkin tortellini, for example. Cibo began his mission after a friend was murdered by extreme nationalists. Food is "more than what we like to eat," he told Vice. "It represents who we are." In his renderings of 'classic Italian dishes', whose origins are more multicultural than might be assumed (basil comes from India, oil is from Syria and tomatoes originate in Colombia), he's sending out an anti-nationalist message that our distant neighbours are really a lot closer than we think.

Meanwhile, in the UK, in Manchester, a series of stickers appeared bearing the image of a tabby and the slogan, "There was some racist rubbish here but I covered it up with this picture of a cat". Originating from an Australian anti-fascist group called 'Cracks Appearing Distro', the stickers have been strategically placed over racist and anti-immigration messages.

And in December 2020, as this book was being written, stickers appeared on lamp posts in Westminster, reading "It's okay to be white" – a slogan adopted by white supremacists and neo-Nazis. After some quick adjustments, they now read, "It's okay". During those impossibly bleak, final days of 2020, it seemed like a quick and easy way of turning hate into hope.

• • • • • • • • • • • • • • • • • • • • • • • • • • •

# I do not ask the wounded person how he feels. I myself become the wounded person.

**Walt Whitman**
(From *Song of Myself*, 1855)

# A shipload of care

How can kindness be manifested during the unfolding of a major disaster?

When the ocean liner Titanic struck an iceberg in the North Atlantic on its maiden voyage from Southampton to New York City in April 1912, the sinking marked one of the 20th century's worst peacetime transport disasters. The Titanic was famously carrying not only some extremely wealthy passengers, there for the luxury of its first-class accommodation, fancy restaurants, libraries and other facilities, but also hundreds of migrants seeking a new life in the United States.

The disaster happened near midnight, and the impact was felt immediately by those on board, although it was some time before the gravity of the situation was fully understood. Women and children were evacuated first, but the Titanic had only 20 lifeboats, many of which were launched half empty. Third-class passengers were largely left to fend for themselves. After two hours, the Titanic suddenly dipped downwards as it filled with water, trapping anyone left below deck. All passengers and crew not already in lifeboats were immersed in lethally cold water. In the early hours of the morning a liner rescued survivors from the lifeboats.

From the traumatised survivors emerged tales of heroism in the line of duty, including wireless operator John Phillips who defied orders to abandon his post and continued to operate SOS. radio equipment, even as the waters rose around him. His body was never recovered.

Chief Steward Andrew Latimer, whose job was to look after first-class passengers, gave his own lifejacket to a female passenger while the Titanic's Captain, Edward Smith, was last seen in the water holding up a child and refusing to abandon his ship. Officer Harold Lowe manned the only available lifeboat to return to the site of the shipwreck, saving six more from the freezing sea.

The Titanic's Liverpudlian Chief Baker Charles Joughin (pronounced 'Jockin') helped women into lifeboats and threw deckchairs into the sea for people to cling to. Assigned to a lifeboat as skipper, he returned to the Titanic at the last moment, not wanting to set a bad example, finally stepping into the sub-zero waters. Incredibly, Joughin survived – perhaps in part thanks to the booze he'd drunk that night. He returned home and lived into his late seventies.

Eyewitnesses also reported acts of selflessness by passengers. Pastor John Harper was a widower travelling with his six-year-old daughter Nana. Having made sure she was safely in a lifeboat, Harper returned to the perilous ship to help others escape. When no more lifeboats could be found he comforted those around with the promise of an afterlife. And when he came across a non-believer, Harper gave the man his own lifejacket, keeping him afloat until he could be rescued. Sadly, Harper succumbed to the icy waves.

Among the first-class passengers on board the Titanic was Noël Leslie, the Countess of Rothes. She knew how to row and, taking the lifeboat's tiller, taught the others on board, encouraging the women to keep their spirits up by singing while they struggled to reach the rescue ship. Once safely on board, the Countess gathered food and medicine for her fellow survivors, translating for those who didn't speak English.

Many men put others first, and several women chose to stay with their men rather than go into the lifeboats. But survivors also reported those who pushed others aside to save themselves, and the lifeboat passengers who avoided capsizing by fending off people struggling in the sea. Of the 2224 people on board, more than 1500 passengers and crew died in the disaster, with only 333 bodies recovered. The story of the Titanic continues to compel as it raises the fundamental question: what would I do in their place?

. . . . . . . . . . . . . . . . . . . . . . . . . . .

Whatever it is you're meant to do, do it now.
The conditions are always impossible.

(Attributed to Doris Lessing)

# A force for good

As millions of acres of land across California, Oregon and Washington State were ravaged by wildfire during September 2020, some 17,000 firefighters were tasked with the seemingly impossible job of getting the inferno under control.

Their unenviable plight deeply affected Sasha Tinning and her five-year-old grandson, Carver. They wanted to do something nice for the firefighters, many of whom were volunteers – just a small gesture of appreciation for these incredibly brave men and women. So they went to the local supermarket with the intention of buying granola bars, nuts and energy snacks to contribute to a donation drive. But on reaching the toy aisle, their eyes fell upon a Baby Yoda doll – the last one on the shelf.

"I said, 'The firefighters could use a friend, couldn't they?'" recalled Tinning. "He would be a very good friend for them," her grandson agreed.

The pair decided the firefighters were very much in need of 'The Force'. They promptly purchased Baby Yoda and dropped him off at a nearby donation station in Oregon, with a note signed by the boy that read, "Thank you firefighters. Here is a friend for you in case you get lonely."

Since then, Baby Yoda has become something of a minor celebrity, with firefighting crews across several states clamouring to take him out on call. The breakout star of Disney's *The Mandalorian* has become an unofficial mascot for the heroic servicemen and women. Sporting a Stars & Stripes bandana, he has attended multiple wildfires, flown in emergency helicopters and administered Covid temperature tests. His Facebook page, 'Baby Yoda Fights Fires' has well over 50,000 followers across the globe, all eagerly awaiting his next adventure. But most importantly, he provides a much-needed morale boost for people working in extremely challenging conditions, who risk their lives for their communities.

How far that little candle throws his beams! So shines a good deed in a naughty world.

**William Shakespeare**
(From *The Merchant of Venice*)

Each one of us has lived through some devastation, some loneliness, some weather superstorm or spiritual superstorm. When we look at each other we must say, "I understand. I understand how you feel because I have been there myself." We must support each other and empathise with each other, because each of us is more alike than we are unalike.

**Maya Angelou**
(Facebook post, 2012)

# Kindness tip

Don't feel the need to
fill a silence. Sitting in
companionable silence,
with someone who needs you
to be with them, can show a
whole lot more kindness
than meaningless platitudes.
And really listen – active
listening is one of the most
underrated skills and it's one
that gets better with practice.
Oh, and always carry tissues.

# Turning kindness up to 11

The music writer John Doran has had quite a ride in his chosen vocation. He's been punched in three separate interviews, and stabbed during two more. But he describes one particular event in 2009 as "the only incident in my career as a journalist that has brought me to tears."

While writing for Metal Hammer magazine, Doran had created a spoof agony uncle called 'Jurgen Toksvig' – "a sexually confused, 19-year-old, church-burning, lunatic Black Metal fan." The joke was very much at the expense of a certain genre throwback: the conspicuously white, unenlightened old-school metaller. "I'm a fan of Black Metal," says Doran, "but I found aspects of it troubling. While it can be very progressive and groundbreaking, at the same time it can be utterly ludicrous."

If metal had previously accrued a bit of a homogenised, heteronormative reputation, by the turn of the century it was becoming ever more tolerant and progressive. The memo had yet to reach 'Jurgen' though – so transparently closeted he'd taken out a green card to Narnia. "He was always talking about feeling very confused when he saw photographs of Metallica with their tops off." None of the letters Jurgen received were hateful or homophobic, however, and he'd even occasionally get positive messages from the LGBTQ+ community, "which was great".

One day, Doran (or his alter-ego) received a letter from a 14- or 15-year-old-teenager. "He was gay and out, and I remember thinking, 'that's a tough town. Hats off to him.' It was a long, rambling email. Maybe he didn't have any other outlet to get this stuff off his chest. He was like, 'I'm out in school, nobody else gets it, I fancy some lad, I get knocked about in the playground and people pick on me.'" Abnormal, they called him. A freak. "That was the bit that stuck in my mind," says John.

By coincidence, Doran was due to interview the lead singer of Judas Priest, Rob Halford, for the following issue. As well as being one of the most innovative and important figures in metal (instantly recognisable in his leather and studs and renowned for his operatic vocals), Halford has the distinction of being the first openly gay metal singer. If his fans call him the Metal God, he has also described himself as "the stately homo of heavy metal".

Before the interview, John was told by Halford's American PR not to bring up his sexuality; that he'd had enough of talking about it. "I decided to ignore her," says Doran. And during the chat, he showed him the teenager's letter. Could Rob possibly pass on a message of support? He certainly could.

"If you could tell that lad that I understand what he's going through and he's not alone," said Halford, whose replies were relayed via Metal Hammer and Doran's own online music magazine, The Quietus. "The same thing happened to me at school. It's a very difficult, painful, lonely experience and you feel like a freak and you ain't. You're perfectly normal – you're ok. All he has to do is to bide his time because once he leaves school, those kids won't be able to touch him and they'll be nowhere. Tell him to stay strong because he'll win in the end."

"I find the whole thing deeply moving," says Doran. "Whatever I feel about Rob Halford as a musician, and I really like Judas Priest, I think what a beautiful human being he must be, to take the time to say that." Doran was contacted by the teenager a few months later. "I heard back from the kid a couple of times. It definitely gave him some confidence. Having one of his heroes, someone really famous in the world of heavy metal, being in his corner – it really gave him something."

• • • • • • • • • • • • • • • • • • • • • • • • • •

If you're really a mean person you're going to come back as a fly and eat poop.

**Kurt Cobain**
(From an interview in Monk magazine, 1992)

# Kindred spirits

In the Irish town of Midleton, County Cork stands Kindred Spirits – a magnificent sculpture, over six metres tall, set against the somewhat incongruous backdrop of Bailick Park. The stainless steel artwork comprises nine giant eagle feathers arranged in a circle, representing a gift of a bowl of food. So what on earth is this demonstrably Native American symbolism doing in Ireland?

Over a seven-year period in the mid-19th century, one million Irish men, women and children died of starvation and disease in one of the deadliest famines in history. About one-eighth of the population perished, and it's estimated that as many as two million people left the country to escape the Potato Famine, never to return.

Donations poured in from all over the world: from Queen Victoria and her servants, the Pope, the Sultan of Turkey, journalists – even prison convicts. And in 1847, at the height of The Great Hunger, the Choctaw Nation gifted the Irish People the sum of $170, equivalent to about $5000 in today's money. While not the biggest donation, not by any stretch, it's certainly one of the most significant.

Just a few years prior, the Native American people had suffered their own privations, having been forcibly removed from their ancestral lands under President Andrew Jackson's Indian Removal Act of 1830. This barbaric act displaced over 100,000 people, forcing them to endure the Trail of Tears, a treacherous journey covering nine states – over 5000 miles. Tens of thousands perished. So this financial gift represented not only a hugely disproportionate sum from a people that had precious little themselves, it was also an incredible act of solidarity – one that Ireland will never forget. The sculpture Kindred Spirits was commissioned to commemorate that act of supreme generosity.

This enduring friendship between the two nations runs deep. In 1992, a group of 22 Irish men and women walked the Trail of Tears, raising $170,000

($1000 for every dollar given in 1847). In 1995, then-President of Ireland, Mary Robinson, travelled to Oklahoma to give thanks. "This gift, so much from those who could afford so little, has given the Choctaw people a unique and cherished place in Irish history, and in the imagination and hearts of our people," she told the crowd. In turn, she was made an honorary chief. In 2018, Irish Taoiseach Leo Varadkar announced The Choctaw-Ireland Scholarship Programme, offering Choctaw scholars full tuition and living expenses for a graduate degree at University College Cork.

The story doesn't end there: at the height of the Covid crisis in 2020, the Choctaw Nation had one of the highest-per-capita infection rates in the world. With inflated rates of asthma, diabetes and obesity being contributing factors, they were incredibly vulnerable to the killer virus. But out of this tragedy came yet another show of unity from their Irish friends. A GoFundMe page set up by Ethel Branch and Cassandra Begay to bring vital resources to Native American communities shielding from Covid saw thousands of donations coming in from Ireland, once again acknowledging the debt. "The people of Ireland stand with our Choctaw Brothers & Sisters," donor Ben O'Leary Fitzpatrick wrote on GoFundMe. "You were there when we were in need, the people of Éire will always stand by you, solidarity with our brothers and sisters. We will never be able to repay the generosity you gave us."

• • • • • • • • • • • • • • • • • • • • • • • • •

The love of neighbour in all its fullness simply means being able to say to him: 'What are you going through?

**Simone Weil**
(From *Waiting on God*, 1951)

To be a revolutionary you
have to be a human being.
You have to care about
people who have no power.

**Jane Fonda**
(From an interview in Newsweek, 1977)

# Kindness tip

Be nice to those working in the service industry, whether it's a waiter or waitress, a shop assistant, a customer service operator or a delivery driver. Anyone. Even if you've experienced bad service. It almost certainly isn't their fault, more likely a systemic failure. Complaining is an art form, and best done from a position of respect and civility. Stick to the facts, try not to get emotional and remain polite. You're far more likely to get a satisfactory outcome.

Also: If you've received good service, leave a good tip.
No excuses.

# The man who returned to Engine Company No. 55

Fans of director Judd Apatow's filthy yet surprisingly sweet comedies were thrilled by his latest movie, 2020's *The King of Staten Island*. It's the story of a still-at-home-with-mom twentysomething slacker who dreams of becoming a tattoo artist, despite his lack of artistic skills. The central role is convincingly played by the film's ungainly co-author, Pete Davidson, based on his own biography. Davidson's father was one of 343 New York firefighters who died during the 9/11 attacks.

On September 12 2001, the day after terrorists hijacked planes and crashed them into the twin towers of the World Trade Center, a "kinda funny-looking" man reported into Engine Company no. 55 in Manhattan's Little Italy, and suited up. He'd been a firefighter there in the 1980s and had left the service to pursue his artistic career, but returned to help with the 9/11 rescue mission.

Alongside other firefighters the volunteer worked 12-hour shifts, digging and sifting through the rubble looking for survivors in the heat and dust. It was arduous work, undertaken only a few months after he'd been stabbed near the eye and in the jaw, throat and arm while bravely intervening in a bar room brawl between movie star Vince Vaughan and locals in Wilmington, North Carolina. The ex-firefighter was Steve Buscemi, better known as an actor in independent films by directors such as Quentin Tarantino, the Coen Brothers and Jim Jarmusch.

Buscemi eschewed all publicity for his 9/11 efforts, refusing photos and interviews, but later explained, "It was a privilege to be able to do it. It was great to connect with the firehouse I used to work with and with some of the guys I worked alongside. And it was enormously helpful for me because while I was working, I didn't really think about it as much, feel it as much."

Nearly 3000 people lost their lives as a result of the 9/11 attacks.

With his fame escalated through a starring role in the television series Boardwalk Empire, Buscemi continued to help the firefighters. He petitioned for better pay and against the closure of fire stations, including Engine Company no. 55, resulting in his arrest at a rally in 2003. And nine years later, at New York's Breezy Point, he quietly helped clean up the devastation wreaked by Super Storm Sandy. These days he also campaigns for Friends of Firefighters, an organisation providing free mental health services to firefighters and their families. As he told *Live with Kelly and Ryan*, the 2020 pandemic was a very "stressful time for first responders in general... it's very hard for them to social distance."

So there's a pleasing symmetry to his casting as a gnarly veteran firefighter named Papa in *The King of Staten Island*, allowing the story of his real-life role in the 9/11 rescue to be retold once again with pride.

• • • • • • • • • • • • • • • • • • • • • • • • • • • •

Even the smallest act of service, the simplest act of kindness, is a way to honour those we lost; a way to reclaim that spirit of unity that followed 9/11.

### Barack Obama
(From the President's Weekly Radio Address, 2011)

## Kindness tip

If you see someone struggling with a heavy load, perhaps a pushchair or big suitcase on a flight of stairs, or at the airport or train station, give them a hand.

Let us learn to show our friendship for a man when he is alive and not after he is dead.

**F Scott Fitzgerald**
(From *The Great Gatsby*, 1925)

# Kindness tip

Random Acts of Kindness Day is held every year on 17 February, and it is massively growing in popularity. Be part of the Kindness Movement: why not buy somebody in the queue behind you a coffee, ask a struggling parent with a stroppy toddler if they're okay, or bake a neighbour a cake. And spread the word about Random Acts of Kindness Day. Kindness is contagious.

# Piano man

One Saturday in July 2020, during one of the most startling, saddest years we'll ever know, a masked man sat down at a piano in a family-owned clearance store in Norwood, Massachusetts and began to play. Before long, a crowd had gathered and were singing along to his impromptu version of Journey's 'Don't Stop Believin''. "Usually, the kids are jumping on it playing 'Chopsticks', which drives everybody nuts," ReMARKable Cleanouts owner Mark Waters told reporters, "so it was good to hear him". Staffer Melissa Rediker filmed him on her phone and uploaded it to ReMARKable's Facebook page. "People wanted to buy it for him and (asked) 'Who was he?'" Alas, she couldn't tell them. As soon as he'd finished, the mystery man was gone.

After the film went viral, Waters decided to gift him the $200 piano. In such extraordinary times, happy endings are truly prized. But how to track the stranger down? Especially when his face was obscured by a pandemic-necessitated mask? The hunt was on. "I thought, 'Is this a good thing or a bad thing that the TV news is looking for me?'" John Capron (for it was he) said later. "I wondered if I might be in some kind of trouble!"

Capron, by his own admission, has "had a somewhat stressful life". After his mother died when he was seven, John, who has only met his biological father once, drifted between foster homes for the next eight years. Following a period living rough, he eventually found a home at a centre for homeless teenagers. While he was there, a counsellor taught him how to play the Journey song on the old in-house upright; a song, incidentally, that a couple of hospitals in Michigan and New York would play years later, whenever a patient had pulled through from Covid. And for a then 15-year-old Capron "something just clicked". Something that gave meaning to his life. "It helps me deal with my emotions," he told the Washington Post. "When I see a piano, I can't help wanting to play it."

By the time he stumbled across the warehouse's piano, the architecture student was living in his own flat and working at Domino's Pizza. By the following week, Waters had managed to locate him. But Waters had changed his mind, too. He wouldn't give John the piano. He was going to give him a precious 1964 Steinway and Sons variety instead, valued at over $3000. "It was clear that he had a lot of talent," said the store owner, "and I had a piano taking up space in my shop. It just made sense to donate it to him."

John, who can't read music and plays by ear, was moved to tears. "I've never owned a piano before, and I couldn't afford one," he said. Before the month was up, the 500 lb Steinway was delivered to his fourth-floor apartment via a crane, free of charge. "If I could, I'd do something like this every day," said Waters. "This country is starving for some good news. [John is] welcome back in the shop any time he likes for a repeat performance."

· · · · · · · · · · · · · · · · · · · · · · · · ·

# I think I have learned that the best way to lift one's self up is to help someone else.

**Booker T Washington**
(From *The Story of My Life and Work, Vol. 1*, 1900)

# Showing the ropes

While the late Captain Tom Moore was doing laps of his Bedfordshire garden during 2020, raising millions of pounds for the NHS and becoming a global sensation in the process, an initially lesser-exposed pensioner was doing similarly amazing work over in his allotment in Harlington, Middlesex. In a series of viral Instagram, Twitter and YouTube videos, 73-year-old Rajinder Singh was using tyres and watering cans as weights, and leaping as if his life depended on it – because millions of other lives did.

At the request of his local temple, or Gurdwara, the retired bus driver, who regularly ran marathons pre-lockdown, had picked up a skipping rope and started jumping, with a stamina that would shame Rocky Balboa. It was Singh's father who'd instilled in his son a love of physical fitness – and a sense of duty, too. Once, while Singh senior was serving in World War II, he had fallen and broken both his ankles. Instead of leaving him to die, as he requested, his fellow soldiers carried the army officer for miles on their backs to safety. It was an example his son never forgot. Years later, he too would find himself helping to fight a different kind of war.

"Exercise is my religion," Rajinder told reporters, who almost immediately dubbed him 'The Skipping Sikh'. Promoting the message that "health is wealth", he encouraged the elderly to keep active during lockdown – particularly his fellow Sikh community who were suffering in isolation due to closure of Gurdwaras during the coronavirus outbreak.

A veteran skipper, the sprightly septuagenarian could muster as many as 5000 jumps in a single day in his sixties. Even now, in his seventies, he can perform an impressive 200 jumps a minute. And to date, he has raised over £14,000 for NHS Charities Together. In June 2020, a "truly humbled" Singh was awarded a Points Of Light award, which recognises outstanding individual volunteers. In October he received an MBE for his services to health and fitness during the pandemic, in the most ethnically diverse Queen's Birthday Honours list ever.

That Christmas – despite not celebrating the festive holiday – he dressed up as Santa Claus (he already has the white beard) and delivered skipping ropes (naturally), chocolate and DVDs to needy children. As his daughter Min Kaur explained, "Our faith says we should show compassion, kindness and love to everyone and my Dad wanted to spread some happiness to children at Christmas."

Rajinder is nothing if not resilient. Back in 1986 he received a telegram from India that his father had been murdered – and had been unable to pay his final respects in person. "Maybe [resilience] is in our blood," Singh told iglobalnews.com. "I think my father and our ancestors are watching over us and blessing us to do more and be something because of their sacrifices."

These days, the man originally hailing from a village called Devidaspura in Punjab can also be found delivering Min's homemade cakes to unsung heroes such as postal workers, supermarket employees, Transport for London staff and elderly neighbours, with the help of his wife and daughter. "I don't want publicity," he told the Guardian. "But if you don't do it, how do people know that you've got a quality that can help others? That's why I'm doing it. And I will carry on until my last breath."

Not all superheroes wear capes. Some wear Santa outfits.

## Kindness tip

If you're fit and able, try a sponsored run for a charity you care about. It doesn't have to be a marathon – just a gentle 5 k will still raise a few quid, and all-important awareness. Alternatively, drag a friend out for a walk. You know, the one who keeps meaning to get some exercise, but never quite gets around to it. We've all got that friend. They might curse you at the time, but deep down, they'll love you for it. Sort of.

# Ducks to water

And now let's take a look at a pair of real-life superheroes: Duck Man and Water Man. First, let's quack on with the former. In 2009, Washington banker Joel Armstrong earned himself the nickname after helping a dozen ducklings to safety. The Sterling Savings loan officer had been monitoring their nest ever since it turned up on a ledge outside his second-floor office window in downtown Spokane. And on Friday 15 May, the guy who'd been pretty handy with a baseball glove in college rocked up at 5 a.m. to catch the befuddled hatchlings as they tottered about and fell off the ledge. A crowd gathered as he expertly caught the first eight. "He's great, a good catcher," a bystander said. "I think Joel's legacy is playing out right here," another nodded approvingly. "The Duck Man." With four flightless birdies still stranded 15 ft above ground level, Armstrong fetched a ladder and carried them down like a fireman, before ushering them in a little waddling conga through the crowded streets and cheering onlookers towards the relative tranquillity of a waiting canal.

On the subject of bringing wildlife to water, here's a bloke who does the opposite. Patrick Kilonzo Mwalua, a pea farmer from Kenya, caught imaginations in 2017 after driving a rented truck for hours each day to bring fresh water to drought-stricken zebra, elephants, antelope and buffalo. Quickly dubbed the 'Water Man', his mission began after he encountered a buffalo sniffing sadly at an empty water hole in Tsavo West National Park. As he'd tell Lifegate.com in 2020, "This really touched my heart. I thought that if it had been me, I could have looked for water somewhere else, but animals can't do this."

With many animals dying or on the brink of dying because of prolonged drought, Patrick decided to intervene. In the face of existing, overcrowded water holes, smaller and younger elephants – already at risk from poachers – were being forced to walk long distances searching for water. "We humans have contributed to climate change, so I decided I needed to take responsibility for them," said Patrick. Although not well off, he spent the little savings he had on hiring a truck to laboriously transport 3000 gallons of fresh water some 50 km to the park – until social media began to take notice, and the funds sluiced in like prayed-for rain, enough for him to buy his own vehicle. At time of writing his GoFundMe page has raised over $450,000.

Nowadays, he's also building dams and new concrete watering holes, while installing solar powered pumps to help animals even further away. Witnesses report elephants and antelopes happily dashing up when they hear the rumble of Patrick's truck with its precious life-giving cargo. "Last night, I found 500 buffalo waiting at the water hole," he told thedodo.com. "They started drinking water while I was standing there. They get so excited."

• • • • • • • • • • • • • • • • • • • • • • • •

He was so benevolent, so merciful a man that, in his mistaken passion, he would have held an umbrella over a duck in a shower of rain.

(Attributed to Douglas William Jerrold)

I mean, I feel like you get more bees with honey.

**Beyoncé Knowles**
(From an interview with Elle.com, 2008)

# Kindness tip

Be kind to nature.
Feed the birds. Create
a Bee Hotel and plant
pollinator-friendly
flowers in the garden.
Try to avoid pesticides.
Don't kill spiders.

# Good korma

Founded in 2010 by cousins Shamil and Kavi Thakrar, the boutique restaurant chain Dishoom was inspired by the Irani cafés of 20th century Bombay. At their peak, these family-run cafes, owned by Zoroastrian immigrants from Iran, were on practically every street corner of the bustling city (corners were considered bad luck, and so property was cheap). Against a backdrop of Partition, the Irani cafés were open to all, providing cheap and wholesome food. Students broke bread alongside solicitors; everyone was welcome, whatever their creed or political persuasion. It is in no small part thanks to these cafés that Bombay remained largely untouched by the horror that ravaged the rest of the country. The Irani cafés brought people together.

That spirit of community lives on in Dishoom and shines through in everything they do. They consistently feature in the Sunday Times '100 Best Companies to Work For'. And in an industry notorious for high staff turnaround and burnout, Dishoom is rightly proud of its record of long-serving staff, and rewards them with a trip to Bombay.

Charity, or 'zakat', is very much at the heart of Dishoom; in 2015 they started supporting two charities, one in the UK and one in India, and for every meal they serve, they donate a meal to a child who would otherwise go hungry. At time of writing, Dishoom have donated over eight million meals. Curry with a conscience.

## Kindness tip

If you know someone going through a tough time, whether it's bereavement or illness, cook a meal for them. All the platitudes in the world can't replace a home-cooked meal. It doesn't have to be fancy or elaborate – just good, wholesome food. Only do this if you can actually cook though, food poisoning would defeat the object. If you can't cook, buy them a cake.

My country is the world,
and my religion is
to do good.

**Thomas Paine**
(From *The Rights of Man*, 1792)

On that best portion
of a good man's life,
His little, nameless,
unremembered acts
Of kindness and of love.

**William Wordsworth**
(From *Lines Written a Few Miles above Tintern Abbey*, 1798)

# Kindness tip

Whether office or home-based, keep a couple of spare umbrellas for colleagues or friends. There's nothing worse than being caught short by unexpected precipitation. Just be prepared that you might not get it back! (Perhaps practice shedding the need for material goods...)

# Heroes of the Holocaust

It's one of the most devastatingly effective moments ever broadcast on television: in 1988, a retired, unassuming English stockbroker called Nicholas Winton was invited to be a member of the audience for the BBC's flagship magazine programme, *That's Life*.

Sir Nicholas was no ordinary banker, in many ways. For starters, he was a devout socialist. Secondly, a segment of the evening was given over to a discussion of how he had smuggled hundreds of endangered children, mainly Jewish, out of Nazi-occupied Czechoslovakia. At one point, presenter Esther Rantzen asked if anyone in the audience who ultimately owed their life to him would stand up – and for their unwitting saviour, who was sitting in the front row, to turn around too. The entire audience stood before him.

Everyone has heard how German industrialist and Nazi Party member Oskar Schindler, at great risk to his own life, saved the lives of 1200 Jews by employing them in his factories (and virtually bankrupting himself via bribes to keep his workers safe). But there were other Schindlers, too, who carried out great acts of courage and selflessness during World War II.

In 1939, Winton helped evacuate 669 children, including future Labour MP Alfred Dubs and filmmaker Karel Reisz, director of *Saturday Night and Sunday Morning*, on the eve of war; rehoming them safely in Britain via what became known as the Czech Kindertransport. Yet having kept schtum about his achievement it slipped under the radar for half a century, until his wife discovered a scrapbook in the attic containing the names of the children and the addresses of their adopters. "I work on the motto that if something's not impossible, there must be a way to do it," he once told *60 Minutes*. He died in 2015, aged 106, and has a planet named after him.

Meanwhile, in 1940, while serving as vice-consul for the Japanese consulate in Kaunas, Lithuania, Chiune Sugihara disobeyed strict instructions from the Tokyo foreign ministry by writing out 2139 transit visas to Jewish refugees to travel via the Soviet Union to Japan, and even the Caribbean. For six weeks during July and August, working round the clock, he directly saved many Polish Jews who'd been displaced by the Soviet invasion. Given that many visa holders were accompanied by a wife and child, the true figure may be closer to 6000, or even 10,000. In common with Winton, Sugihara remained low-key about his actions until they were uncovered decades later. Saving people's lives was simply the "right thing to do," he said.

While the rest of the world was at war, India was engaged in its own battle – struggling to remove the stranglehold of British colonialism, while also suffering through famine and drought. In 1942, an 'Indian Oskar Schindler' took in 1000 Jewish and Catholic orphans from Poland, refugees from the 1939 Soviet invasion, after the British governor refused to allow them off their ship at Bombay. Their benefactor, Digvijaysinhji Ranjitsinhji Jadeja of Nawanagar – a real-life Maharaja, no less – became known as 'our Bapu' ('father'), after he allowed the ship to enter his own port at Rosi. "Do not consider yourself orphans," he told them as they disembarked. You are now Nawnagaris and I am Bapu, father of all the people of Nawanagar, so also yours."

Tents were supplied, a party was thrown, and a children's camp was set up in Balachadi near Bapu's summer palace, with meals prepared by cooks from Goa. And as the Brits fumed about the new influx, the Maharaja drew up adoption certificates for them, proudly proclaiming them members of his own family. He even organised football matches. As survivor Wieslaw Stypula told makers of the 2015 Indo-Polish documentary *A Little Poland in India*, "When we won, the Maharaja rose up from his armchair, stood smiling and clapping, almost as if it mattered to him that the match had ended in a victory for these newcomers from a distant country, than for his own countrymen."

It's difficult in times like these; ideals, dreams and cherished hopes rise within us, only to be crushed by grim reality. It's a wonder I haven't abandoned all my ideals, they seem so absurd and impractical. Yet I cling to them because I believe, in spite of everything, that people are truly good at heart.

**Anne Frank**
(From *The Diary of a Young Girl*, 21 July 1944)

# Kindness tip

Try to see the good in people.
If someone is lashing out
or behaving badly, there's
probably a root cause.
Most people are inherently
good. Perhaps they don't
realise the effect of their words
or actions. Or perhaps they are
going through a tough time.
Put yourself in their shoes,
and whatever you do,
don't go tit for tat.

# Hail Caesar

Llamas have a notoriously bad reputation for being aggressive. Not so Caesar McCool, the self-proclaimed 'No Drama Llama'. The former Grand Champion show llama turned 'Llamactivist' has become a celebrity in his hometown of Portland, Oregon, providing emotional support hugs to those that need them most. A veteran of over 50 civil rights and environmental events, including the Black Lives Matter protests of summer 2020, Caesar helps reduce tensions during what can potentially become incredibly volatile situations.

Standing at 5'8" and weighing 350 lb, the native Argentine causes quite the stir wherever he goes, attracting legions of fans on his Instagram account (nearly 13,000 followers at time of writing). Caesar's owner Larry McCool has cared for dozens of llamas at his Mystic Llama Farm in Jefferson, Oregon, but he knew Caesar was something special from the get-go. "He's a magical creature," McCool told the Washington Post. "I wish I could take some credit for him, but he's developed all on his own. I've been his tutor and his guide, but sometimes I'm the one following him."

Despite working in often extremely challenging, highly charged circumstances, and once narrowly escaping being tear-gassed, Larry has never felt that he or Caesar were in any great danger. "They'll be clapping, chanting, stomping, and all of a sudden I'll get up with Caesar and the next thing I know, everyone will just band around him." He continued, "I don't care how big, how staunch, how intense that somebody is – it could be a big marcher in total riot gear, and he will come up and give Caesar a big hug."

When he's not being an ally, Caesar spends his spare time visiting the elderly in nearby retirement homes. Providing positivity, comfort, laughter and smiles wherever he goes, Caesar is never afraid to put his neck on the line.

I would like to be known as a person who is concerned about freedom and equality and justice and prosperity for all people.

**Rosa Parks**
(Said upon her 77th birthday)

# Kindness tip

Offer your seat on public transport to someone that needs it more than you.
And remember, the need isn't always immediately obvious.

# Two acts of kindness

These are two incidents that happened to this book's co-author Ali Catterall and his mum, 40 years apart. Both are characterised by acts of supreme generosity. But did one act impact upon the very fabric of space and time itself?

In the late summer of 1971, when Ali was a one-year-old, he and his mum were hitchhiking in a van across Greece. One night their route was blocked by an entire village of people dancing in the road. "Join us!" they cried, and everyone piled out into the kind of adventure no money could buy. But the dancing and wine meant they couldn't go much further, so they steered into a tomato field just outside town to sleep. While the van owners slept in the back, Ali and his mum bedded down among the tomatoes. By morning they were both covered with mosquito bites. As they limped back to the van, they were stopped by an elderly woman, who approached them with a can of milk. "I heard the child crying in the night," she said, in English. "Please take this for him."

Her name was "Annie – Anastasia", she said. She'd learned English from soldiers during the war. Her house, just across the road from the field, was scarcely bigger than the van and constructed from beaten-out paraffin cans. The can of milk must have cost her a day's food – maybe more. Yet she pressed it on them with smiles, these people she'd never met and would almost certainly never meet again.

Decades later, in October 2011, Ali's mum was travelling in Jordan, when, due to a mix-up, she ended up in a different hotel from the one she'd originally booked. She stayed for a night – enough time to befriend the owner, Hazel, who had a bad back. As Ali's mum has some medical expertise, she gave her some physio for it, and left the following morning, catching a taxi back to the airport.

Rewind.

The previous August, thousands of miles away, Ali was taking an endless cycle ride into oblivion, to get over a relationship split. One night, returning from Walton-on-Thames, some 15 miles from home, his old iron war horse of a bike finally gave up the ghost and died. At 4 am. A long way from London. He was distraught. The streets were deserted. If a cab didn't come along, and soon, it was going to be a five or six hour walk back to town.

Fast-forward.

In November, Hazel, who was visiting London, treated Ali's mum to lunch, to thank her for the physio. Over the course of the meal, they exchanged some family details, and what have you.

Rewind.

Back in Kingston, back in August, Ali finally flagged down the only black cab prepared to stop and help ferry the wretched contraption back to the capital. It was a kindly, middle-aged Middle-eastern man, and as it was a long-ish journey back, they got chatting; about their lives, families and careers. As he dropped Ali to his door, the driver, whose name was Ibrahim, accepted the only thing Ali had in his pocket: a couple of quid – significantly less than the actual fare would have been – then spent the next half-hour attempting to fix the bike himself in the road, gamely muddying his hands on the greasy chain.

Fast-forward. Late-November 2011.

Ali's mum received an email from Hazel. The week before, while chatting with her husband, who occasionally worked in London as a taxi driver, she mentioned Ali's mum and Ali to him. And Ibrahim suddenly exclaimed, "This is crazy, but I think that's the guy I picked up last August."

Sometimes, the kindest people are those we meet along the way – those who give us their hearts and ask nothing in return. Then, when the opportunity presents itself, even if it's years later, we pass it on.

• • • • • • • • • • • • • • • • • • • • • • • •

## We're all just walking each other home.

(Attributed to Ram Dass)

I think that it was
Ben Jonson who said,
I have studied all the
theologies and all
the philosophies,
but cheerfulness keeps
breaking through.

**Leonard Cohen**
(From an interview in The Daily Telegraph, 1993)

# Kindness tip

Smile and say "hello" to random strangers. It's good for you! The physical act of smiling reduces blood pressure, lowers stress levels and improves your mood. And it burns more calories (relatively) than frowning. And you'll probably get a nice smile back in return.

# Grist to the mills

Life for workers during the British Industrial Revolution was more or less Hell on Earth – 14- or 16-hour days, six days a week. Employees were often paid in tokens that were worthless outside the factory, and they used these to pay for terrible, overpriced in-house goods. Horribly maimed workers were fired if they couldn't keep up.

If hazardous machinery, flammable liquids, collapsing buildings and a raft of diseases killed off many employees in those dark Satanic mills, there was always an inexhaustible supply of sallow, sunken-eyed five-or-six-year-olds from the local workhouses to replace them. Witness reports describe children as stunted, half-clothed... "No human beings can be more wretched."

If the Health and Morals of Apprentices Act 1802 tried to limit children's working hours, it was rarely enforced. In 1815, a Welsh textile manufacturer named Robert Owen drafted a bill banning the employment of children under 10, plus the implementation of a two-hour lunch break and half an hour's school lessons. The Bill that passed four years later was a very pale shadow of it. But Owen was just getting warmed up.

Robert Owen was rich. He was also a proto-socialist, who dreamed of a workers' Utopia. Owen believed society formed people's character. He thought that if people were placed in better conditions, and treated with kindness, it would create a kinder society – one that worked more productively too.

To demonstrate the scope of his achievements, it's worth setting them out chronologically. This is just a fraction: back in 1810 he'd instituted an eight-hour day at his New Lanark mills ("enough for any human being"). In 1812, he organised an early furlough scheme, continuing to pay wages during the War of 1812, when the mills were closed for four months during an embargo against the US. In 1816, he founded the world's first infant school at New Lanark, the Institute for the Formation of Character. Along with teaching subjects such as reading, writing, maths and history, it placed an equal emphasis on character development, and banned Bible lessons and corporal punishment – even "harsh critical words". Children were encouraged to sing, dance and play.

By 1817 he'd completely rejected organised religion, including the Church of England, and argued for a "new moral world... from which the bitterness of divisive sectarian religion would be banished", further attributing the national and economic malaise not only to the aftermath of the Napoleonic Wars but to the competition of human labour with machinery. "Eight hours labour, eight hours recreation and eight hours rest," he insisted.

By 1824 he'd invested a chunk of his fortune in an experimental socialist commune in Indiana which he named 'New Harmony' (admittedly, this lasted all of two years). Returning to London, he developed co-operative movements, supported the trade union movement, free education drives, free museums and public libraries and social reform in women's rights. "Women will be no longer made the slaves of, or dependent upon, men," he wrote in 1841. "They will be equal in education, rights, privileges and personal liberty."

Among the ideas he installed at New Lanark were free education for all, including adult evening classes, a crèche for working mums, free basic healthcare and a shorter working week. He improved the workers' filthy, overcrowded slums, stocked the factory store with decent goods at affordable prices, and fed the profits back into the community. "Do you regret having wasted your life on fruitless ideas?" he was asked on his deathbed by a church minister, probably still peeved at Owen's attitude to Christianity. "My life was not useless," Owen replied. "I gave important truths to the world, and it was only for want of understanding that they were disregarded. I have been ahead of my time."

• • • • • • • • • • • • • • • • • • • • • • • • • •

Do the wise thing and the kind thing too,
and make the best of us and not the worst.

**Charles Dickens**
(From *Hard Times*, 1854)

Policies don't require human beings to care about other human beings. Though it is morally right.

**Kamala Harris**
(Interviewed in Elle magazine, 2015)

# Kindness tip

Be an ally. Speak up.
Use your voice to help the
marginalised, be it through
peaceful protests, signing
petitions or writing to your MP
or Government Representative.
Change can happen, but only
if we work together.

# All you have to do is call

Loneliness is a Silent Killer. It has long been associated with problems such as substance abuse, depression and eating disorders. Moreover, chronic loneliness is comparable to smoking 15 cigarettes a day, and according to several studies may be more damaging to health than obesity. Combine loneliness with another Silent Killer, namely Covid-19, and the effects can be devastating, especially to older members of the community forced into isolation.

The UK-based care home group 'Creating Happiness Daily' recognised this and took action. They set up an Adopt a Grandparent scheme whereby individuals were buddied up with care home residents for regular phone/video chats, and even old-school letters. "The idea behind it was to promote inter-generational communication and the relationship between children and older people, which is very valuable," a CHD Living spokesperson told the Independent.

What began life as a local initiative quickly went viral – over 72,000 virtual volunteers have now signed up from all over the world, ranging from ages one (!) to 76. Pairings are carefully matched to ensure there are common interests, and each call is overseen by a supervisor. It has proved to be hugely rewarding for all parties involved. Rosie Kirkin, a sprightly 88-year-old was paired with volunteer Anika Brandt, who had recently lost both her grandparents. "In times like these, we've got to be kind and help each other and realise how necessary it is to reach out and be close emotionally," Rosie told Sky News. Rosie and Anika very much hope to meet in real life once the pandemic has passed, and it is safe to do so.

In 2015, the Soto del Real library in Madrid started Bibliotherapy for the Elderly. Headed up by librarian Juan Sobrino, he and a band of volunteers visited elderly locals in care homes approximately once a month to read to them. When Covid hit, that was no longer an option due to social distancing regulations, so they quickly pivoted. The Tales on the Phone service was launched, providing weekly phone calls to elderly residents instead. It has been a huge hit. Volunteers read from books, recite poetry and even read plays. But, crucially, they form a relationship with their elderly charges and provide a much-needed connection to the outside world. As Sobrino told El Pais about Olvido, one of his clients,

"I read a lot of poetry to him because he likes it a lot. When I read him poems by Machado, he begins to tell me about the places he remembers."

Meanwhile, PetsTogether.org provides virtual 'chats' with pets (and their owners) to help people stay socially connected and engaged – especially older people living in nursing homes, assisted living centres or staying in hospital. The New York-based non-profit Animal Farm Foundation offers free calls with a range of animals including a horse called Marcus, Kapow! the dog (exclamation mark included), Muffin and Baby the cows and Smudge the cat. The organisation firmly believes in the healing power of animals, but perhaps even more importantly, the humans are forming bonds too, providing vital connections. As to what the future holds in a post-Covid world, they very much hope to continue their good work, stating on their website: "We hope that the program will endure even after this time of social distancing is over. Feelings of isolation and loneliness existed before Covid-19 and will still exist after. We'll always be here to help."

• • • • • • • • • • • • • • • • • • • • • • • •

...And the good news is, kindness is catching. If you are unilaterally kind, research has shown that it is likely that your partner will catch it and pass it on.

**Philippa Perry**
(From *The Book You Wish Your Parents Had Read*, 2019)

## Kindness tip

Make sure you stay in regular contact with elderly or frail relatives/friends. Chances are they mightn't have spoken to another person all day, and just a single call once a day will mean the world to them.

Very little is off-limits,
but draw the line at
being unkind.

**RuPaul**
(From *RuPaul's Drag Race: Reunion*)

# Kindness tip

Regardless of your gender, be part of the Sisterhood. Lift women up, don't drag them down. Encourage them. Praise them. Celebrate them. Don't reduce them to their looks or size. Don't see women as competition, unless you're a competitive sportswoman – in which case it's fine.

# The hounds of love

October 2020: amid howling winds, and with Category 2 storm Hurricane Delta incoming, Ricardo Pimental, owner of Mexico's Tierra de Animales Sanctuary, which gives a new leash of life to dogs rescued from dogfighting rings and abuse, wrote a Facebook update. "We have already started the preparation work for the hurricane, cutting branches, securing things that can fly, walling up windows and doors, filling drums with water, charging flashlight batteries etc." More radically, like a latter-day Noah, he was going to herd the Sanctuary's animals into his own house, "so there is going to be a poop party. But what can you do?" Showing dogged determination, he turned his home over to 300-plus dogs, dozens of cats, rabbits and even a hedgehog.

The viral post brought in thousands of donations, and Pimental was soon hounded by the media. "It doesn't matter if the house smells dirty, it can be cleaned," he told Associated Press. "The things they broke can be fixed or bought again, but what's beautiful is to see them happy, healthy and safe, without wounds and the possibility of getting adopted." There was significant damage to the Sanctuary – the roof was even torn off the shelter. But all the animals survived the night, thanks to his pawsitive action.

Meanwhile in Italy, a branch of IKEA gave a whole new meaning to the term 'let sleeping dogs lie'. In 2018, the Sicilian town of Catania saw two weeks of torrential rain and flooding. It was literally raining cats and dogs. Kind-hearted IKEA staff allowed stray dogs into the store, letting them sleep on the rugs among the furnishings, to the delight of locals. One customer told The Dodo: "What an absolutely fantastic thing to do! Showing such compassion to these poor creatures is a fine example to us all." Some lucky pooches even found new homes as a result. Incidentally, this isn't the first time man's best friend has been given a helping paw by the Scandinavian furniture chain, who once partnered with an animal charity to encourage adoption. Life-sized cardboard cut-outs of cats and dogs were placed around its stores, containing barcode links to further information on how to adopt. No self-assembly required.

Similarly, a New York pizzeria had a pawsome idea. Working with the Society for the Prevention of Cruelty to Animals, the Just Pizza & Wings Co in Amherst attached photos of adoptable dogs to delivery boxes in the hope of finding forever homes, offering $50 gift certificates to anyone who snapped one up. This purveyor of pupperoni pizzas takes thinking outside the box to a whole new level.

Not to be outdone, Fido's Taphouse bar in Portland, Oregon doubles-up as a foster home for pups rescued from kill shelters. Typically housing three or four dogs at any one time, they've successfully re-homed over 70 of them. With the motto "Eat. Drink. Adopt", owner Scott Porter hopes they'll bring the same therapeutic support his pets have given him: "My own dogs helped me through some pretty severe depression," he told TODAY.com. "They were extremely loving and attentive to me. And they understood that I was going through some tough times." And fear not, those concerned about adopting under the influence of alcohol: Fido's Taphouse operates a very strict policy, requiring a three-day wait before signing the paperwork. Now that's what we call the hair of the dog.

• • • • • • • • • • • • • • • • • • • • • • • • •

# Kindness. The only possible method when dealing with a living creature.

**Mikhail Bulgakov**
(From *The Heart of a Dog*, 1925)

# One simple handshake

On 29 July 1981, nearly one billion people across the globe tuned in to watch the wedding of HRH Prince Charles and Lady Diana Spencer. A star was born: a modern princess, with a playful sense of humour and real emotional intelligence. Compassionate and down to earth, with essentially relatable problems, she struck a chord with so many that Tony Blair's 'the People's Princess' tag seems pretty justified in retrospect. (Can you imagine how devastatingly cool she'd be today, had she lived? Taking no prisoners on Twitter and living her best life?)

Around the same time as the Royal Wedding, reports began trickling in of a killer disease, a 'cancer' apparently targeting the gay community. Fast-forward to the mid-1980s, and hysteria surrounding the so-called "gay plague" was at fever pitch. Misinformation was rife and the community was under constant threat – from the media, the public and of course the virus itself. Already one of the most vulnerable, marginalised groups, they were now social pariahs. Driven by fear and ignorance, tabloid headlines such as "I'd shoot my son if he had AIDS" (and that was from a vicar) were commonplace.

Diana was no stranger to charitable good deeds. As a working Royal, she was attached to over 100 charities. It was her obligation, and she did it with great aplomb. As arguably the most famous woman on the planet, she wielded huge power and influence, and she knew it.

On 19 April, 1997, Diana opened the Broderip Ward for HIV/AIDS victims at London's Middlesex Hospital. It was the first purpose-built unit of its kind in the country, accommodating 12 patients. None of them had been willing to be photographed with her, fearing more bad press and repercussions. But Ivan Cohen, a terminally ill 32-year-old, did agree – under cover of anonymity, and with the request that he was photographed from behind, such was the stigma. What happened next made history. In front of the world's media, an un-gloved Diana shook his hand. A small, simple, bold deed that sent shockwaves around the world. "HIV does not make people dangerous to know," she told press, "so you can shake their hand and give them a hug. Heaven knows they need it."

It is impossible to overestimate how much that act and those words changed public perception. A close friend of Diana's, and founder of the eponymous AIDS Foundation (which has donated over $450 m to projects and saved five million lives), Sir Elton John would reiterate its importance during a 2018 HIV lecture. "One simple handshake, one gesture showed the world the desperate need for humanity for people living with AIDS. She knew the disease could not be communicated by hand. Her gesture meant nobody should be left behind. She did not distinguish between 'us' and 'them'."

Diana scaled back on charitable duties towards the end of her life, but remained a Patron of the National AIDS Trust up until her death in 1997, and was a regular visitor to the London Lighthouse AIDS charity. "In our opinion, Diana was the foremost ambassador for AIDS awareness on the planet," Gavin Hart of the National AIDS Trust told the BBC. "No one can fill her shoes in terms of the work she did."

These days, Diana's legacy lives on through her son Harry, Duke of Sussex. In 2016, he took two HIV tests, live on camera. On World AIDS Day during a trip to Barbados, he roped in Rihanna, in the hope of reaching out to her millions of fans, showing just how quick and easy the finger prick test is. "I want to say to everyone who hasn't been tested – get tested, regardless of who you are, your background, culture or religion," he said.

It is estimated that some 38 million people worldwide are living with HIV, and at time of writing over 35 million people have died of AIDS-related illnesses. There is still so much work to be done.

# Anything else just isn't cricket

Balmy summer afternoons. Cream teas. The sound of leather on willow. Cricket: the gentleman's game. But is it really? Suffice to say, not all cricketers are gentlemanly, and rivalry is fierce. Stories about 'sledging' are rife – that is, the tactic of insulting or verbally assaulting the opposing player in the hope of upsetting their concentration and causing them to make mistakes. Sledges can be deeply personal, are sometimes viciously funny, often family related, and, on occasion, even threaten to bring matches to the brink of physical violence.

Perhaps one of the least offensive examples of sledging is an incident that occurred between the legendary West Indian batsman Viv Richards and the young Welsh fastbowler Greg Thomas. After Richards had repeatedly missed the ball, Thomas walked down the pitch and told him, "I'll give you a clue. It's round, it's red, it's made of leather and it's got a seam on it." Richards hit the next ball out of the stadium.  Then he walked up the pitch and said to Thomas, "You know what it looks like, maybe you should go and find it."

Arguably the fiercest rivalry is between England and Australia in The Ashes test cricket series, held every two years. The teams play for a *ridiculously* tiny trophy, standing just 10.5 cm tall. But more than that, they play to settle scores that have been brewing for 150 years.

Summer 2005 saw one of the closest fought Ashes ever: Australia was ranked #1 in the world, and England were very much the underdogs, not having won the *ludicrously* diminutive prize for 18 years. But during that most nail-biting of tours, the tables were turned. And on day four of the second test at Edgbaston, England claimed a victory that would all but guarantee them the *impossibly teeny-weeny* cup. The tourists were *devastated*, not least Brett Lee, a fast bowler who had fought valiantly. As the rest of the England team celebrated, Andrew 'Freddie' Flintoff took the time to console a visibly distressed Lee, who was crouched on his haunches in despair, laying a supportive hand on his shoulder. This fleeting moment was to become one of the most famous ever images of sportsmanship. "We'd just beat them and he'd done really well and I like Brett Lee and he was crying," Flintoff recalled for UK game show *A League of their Own*. "I said, 'Mate, this is embarrassing... you've lost, it's cricket, nobody cares, the trophy's (tiny), f***ing get over it – it really does not matter'."

The writers of this book can't lay claim to knowing our googlies from our dibbly dobblys. But we do know a kind act when we see one.

• • • • • • • • • • • • • • • • • • • • • • • • • • • •

No one needs to teach you to be mean; we need to be taught to be kind.

**Nikki Giovanni**
(From an interview in artvoice.com, 2008)

## Kindness tip

Do hold doors open for people. And when someone does the same for you, please remember to thank them. (Politeness is free. Always say "Please" and "Thank You".)

# Mary's promise

One afternoon in Victorian England, an RSPCA member called Mary Tealby paid a visit to a friend, Sarah Major, who lived in Canonbury Square. As fate would have it, rather than being ushered into the drawing room, she was shown into the kitchen. There, she found a tiny emaciated dog Sarah had rescued, literally, from the gutter. Tealby carried it home and sat with it the entire night, feeding it a teaspoon of warm port every hour. Sadly, it died in the morning. But that day, she vowed never to ignore a dog in need. And because of this, Battersea Dogs and Cats Home call their mission 'Mary's promise': "To do whatever it takes to make sure we never turn away a dog or cat that needs our help."

Dogs haven't always been man's best friend, at least where the British are concerned. Prior to the Victorian era, the phrase "It's a dog's life" couldn't have been more apt: they were randomly shot for sport, forced into dogfights or stoned in the streets. It was the likes of Queen Victoria and noted dog lover Charles Darwin who helped promote kindness towards animals per se, to the point where Greyfriars Bobby and Black Beauty became such sentimental 19th century figures.

Battersea Dogs and Cats Home actually began in Islington, North London, when Tealby founded her 'canine asylum', the Home for Lost and Starving Dogs in 1860, in what became Chillingworth Road in Lower Holloway. Initially, she was met with scorn, even disgust, for taking in stray dogs off the street at a time when they were made to pull carts until they dropped dead. Locals mounted court cases because of the noise. Even the Times newspaper stuck the boot in. "When we hear of a 'Home for Dogs' we venture to doubt if the originators and supporters of such an institution have taken leave of their sober senses," it thundered. By running a shelter for homeless hounds, when there were more deserving homeless humans, she was "letting her zeal outrun her discretion". Back then, the concept of an upper-middle class woman – a divorcee no less – offering even "temporary rescue" to things that were considered vermin was incredibly strange, even scandalous.

In the beginning, Tealby relied on fundraisers and donations from friends like Major to power the home, which later added local stables. And then Charles Dickens sat up and noticed. "It is the kind of institution," he wrote in 1862 of Mary's dog house, "which a very sensitive person who has suffered acutely from witnessing the misery of a starving animal would wish for, without imagining for a moment that it would ever seriously exist. It does seriously exist, though." A colossus of the 19th century, Dickens' impact cannot be understated, from his influence on social reform to how we think about Christmas. His priceless patronage considerably helped raise the home's reputation, to the point where Queen Victoria became its patron.

By the close of the century, animal sanctuaries were becoming commonplace, thanks to the trail blazed by Tealby. The Home moved to Battersea in 1871, when it also started taking in cats – it officially changed its name in 2002 to reflect its more diverse intake. Since then, the charity has rescued, reunited and rehomed more than 3.1 million cats and dogs with (carefully vetted) humans. But not before they're given a thorough veterinary check, and surgery if needed, then vaccinated, neutered and microchipped. Over the years it has run numerous public awareness campaigns, including 2019's "Rescue Is My Favourite Breed" – a drive to encourage more people to adopt. This story is dedicated to one of those rescue pets, Ghost 'Ghostie' Buxton, a British shorthair, and her adoptive mum Clare, a British longhair, among the many beneficiaries of Mary Tealby's amazing legacy.

• • • • • • • • • • • • • • • • • • • • • • • • •

## Our perfect companions never have fewer than four feet.

(Attributed to Colette)

# Little helpers

By late May 2020, the mystery illness that many people had become dimly aware of via strange stories about docked cruise liners, had brought the world to its knees. Yet by acting swiftly, a handful of countries such as Taiwan, Fiji and Norway (which has notably low levels of government corruption) managed to flatten the curve much quicker than others. Chief among these countries was New Zealand, which at time of writing has shown Covid the door not once, but twice. This is in no small part down to the decisive actions of prime minister Jacinda Ardern, whose strict lockdowns (at the time, the strictest in the world) and closed borders all but eliminated the pandemic in New Zealand early on. Even at peak-infection, just 89 cases were recorded daily in the land Sam Neill and Dame Kiri Te Kanawa call home, compared with the UK's 60,000 a day (one in 50 people) by January 2021.

But that's not the only reason to salute twice-elected Jacinda. In April 2020, she announced the addition of two essential workers to the list of people who had freedom to go about their crucial supply business during national lockdown. "You'll be pleased to know that we do consider both the Tooth Fairy and the Easter Bunny to be essential workers," she told a coronavirus news briefing after young Kiwis had raised concerns. However, she stressed that their deliveries might be a little impeded: "If the Easter Bunny doesn't make it to your household, then we have to understand that it's a bit difficult at the moment for the bunny to perhaps get everywhere… as you can imagine, at this time they're going to be potentially quite busy at home with their family as well and their own bunnies."

Other world leaders hopped to it. Following a video query from a seven-year-old girl called Raphaelle, Quebec Premier François Legault also declared the Tooth Fairy a key worker – and immune to coronavirus, too, which makes sense as fairies are a different species. Meanwhile, Guernsey's Director of Public Health, Dr Nicola Brink, confirmed that a certain jolly old man would receive full essential worker status at Christmas, drawing on evidence that there was no coronavirus at the North Pole. "We're delighted to announce today that Father Christmas has been given critical worker status," she reassured press. "He will be subject to no isolation, no testing, and will be able to visit us freely."

That November, Irish MP Simon Coveney stressed that Saint Nick wouldn't be subject to the usual travel restrictions when he flew in the following month. "As Minister for Foreign Affairs we've been working on the Santa Claus issue for a number of weeks now," he revealed. "It's important to say to all children in the country that we regard his travels as essential travel for essential purposes and therefore he is exempt from the need to self-quarantine for 14 days and should be able to come in and out of Irish airspace and indeed in and out of Irish homes without having to restrict his movement." However, he also emphasised that children were to remain in their beds during his visit – for socially distanced reasons, of course.

• • • • • • • • • • • • • • • • • • • • • • • • • • • •

It takes courage and strength to be empathetic... I am trying to chart a different path, and that will attract criticism but I can only be true to myself and the form of leadership I believe in.

**Jacinda Ardern**
(From an interview with BBC News, 2018)

# Chadwick pays it forward

In August 2020, the world reeled from the news that *Black Panther* star Chadwick Boseman had died from stage IV colon cancer at the age of 43. In *Black Panther* – the biggest-grossing film of all time from a black director, led by an almost exclusively black cast – he played T'Challa, the eponymous future King of Wakanda. But as tributes poured in from the world of showbiz, stories started to emerge which demonstrated just how much of a king he really was. The truth is, he'd kept his diagnosis secret for years – and had bagged his biggest roles only after he became ill. The likes of *Marshall*, *Da 5 Bloods*, *Ma Rainey's Black Bottom* – and yes, *Black Panther* (for which he performed his own stunts) – had been filmed between bouts of chemotherapy, and nobody had been the wiser.

Boseman had another secret: as he told the 47th AFI Lifetime Achievement Award ceremony, its recipient, Denzel Washington, had been asked by former *Cosby Show* star Phylicia Rashad to assist her in privately funding nine students from Howard University for a summer acting programme at the UK's British American Drama Academy. "As fate would have it, I was one of the students that he paid for," Boseman told the audience. "Imagine receiving the letter that your tuition for that summer was paid for and that your benefactor was none other than the dopest actor on the planet?" When Chadwick finally met him at the New York City premiere of *Black Panther*, Washington grinned, "Oh so that's why I'm here? You owe me money. I came to collect!"

That same February 2018, he paid for a screening of the film for 312 underprivileged kids at the Amstar theatre in his hometown of Anderson, South Carolina. Two years later, his *21 Bridges* co-star, Sienna Miller, revealed how he'd donated part of his salary to give her financial parity for her role, after the studio refused to meet her pay request. As Miller told Empire, it was the sort of generosity and support that was all too rare in the film industry. "[It] just doesn't happen. He said, 'You're getting paid what you deserve, and what you're worth.' It's just unfathomable to imagine another man in that town behaving that graciously or respectfully... But there was no showiness, it was, 'Of course I'll get you to that number, because that's what you should be paid'. It was the most astounding thing that I've experienced."

Meanwhile, Trevor Reece, a former clerk at LA's Samuel French Film & Theater bookshop, revealed that Boseman had once quietly stopped by his bookstore, where a young black actor had approached him and engaged him in conversation for over half an hour. Chadwick had taken the time to give him industry advice, before picking out some books for the actor, paying for them and asking Trevor to hold them behind the counter for him. "He didn't want thanks," Trevor told Twitter. "He just wanted to make sure this young man was taken care of and had access to resources he would need to succeed... Chadwick Boseman was the King of Wakanda. He was James Brown and Jackie Robinson. But above all that, he was a good man."

• • • • • • • • • • • • • • • • • • • • • • • • • •

I'd like for them to say: "He took a few cups of love. He took one tablespoon of patience, one teaspoon of generosity, one pint of kindness. He took one quart of laughter, one pinch of concern. And then, he mixed willingness with happiness."

**Muhammed Ali**
(From an interview with David Frost, 1974)

# Greeks bearing gifts

University student and extreme sports fan Eleftheria Tosiou had a Herculean ambition. She wanted to reach the top of Mount Olympus, home of the Greek Gods. And as a lifelong wheelchair user, she had just the person in mind to help her.

Marios Giannakou is a long-distance endurance runner, hailing (like Eleftheria) from the somewhat appropriately named town of Drama in north-eastern Greece. In addition to completing several ultramarathons, including a 160-mile hike in the Al Marmoom Desert and winning a 93-mile race in Antarctica, he's previously scaled the notoriously slippery, 2917-metre-high mountain no less than 50 times. But his 51st climb would be the most significant. As he'd later tell press, "All international races, medals and distinctions so far mean little compared to that goal."

Having met the biology student through a mutual friend, he immediately agreed to her request. And though not quite a Sisyphean task, it nonetheless presented a particular set of challenges. He and an assembled team knew they had to act swiftly to ferry Eleftheria safely to the throne of Zeus, before the snows arrived. But he had a potential Achilles heel. "The most difficult part was the psychological one," he said. "A man lost his life there a day before."

On 5 October, 2020, a month after the pair first met, he began the 10-hour descent, carrying Tosiou on his shoulders in a specially adapted backpack, pausing with guides to set up camp and have a bit of a rest halfway up. "At 09:02 a.m. we reached the top of Greece," he wrote on Instagram. "There is nothing more real than the dream." Greek Prime Minister Kyriakos Mitsotakis later congratulated the pair via a video call. "I was happy, I was moved," said Tosiou. "In the end it was most intense when we came down, and realised what we had done." Added Giannakou, "I have never done something more beautiful. I think it has completed me as a person." And maybe centaured him, too.

Three things in human life are important. The first is to be kind. The second is to be kind. And the third is to be kind.

(Attributed to Henry James)

## Kindness tip

Be kind to the planet. There are dozens of quick and easy lifestyle changes that you can make, and they will probably save you money, too. Turn the thermostat down by one degree. Always turn your laptop or PC off at night and, when printing, use an ink-saving font such as Century Gothic. (On the subject of printing, consider opting for paper-free bills.) Eat less meat. Recycle and re-use. Buy second-hand. Walk or use public transport wherever possible. These are all relatively small tweaks, but cumulatively, they make a difference.

# The cat's pyjamas

Cats have a bit of a rep for being standoffish and self-interested (lies, wicked, wicked lies). But one particular resident of a Polish animal shelter certainly puts paid to that purrrfectly outrageous notion.

In 2015, the world was alerted to the story of a 'nurse cat', who "cuddles animals back to health". Given up for adoption at two months old, and suffering a contagious upper respiratory infection, the little black kitten was thought to be a goner when he fetched up at the doors of the Schronisko dla Zwierząt hospital in Bydgoszcz during autumn 2014.

"He was in a terrible state and I decided that the best thing for him would be to put him down to end his suffering," shelter vet Lucyna Kuziel-Zawalich told Polish news channel TVN24. "Maybe he knew he was near the end and began fighting for his life. Whatever, he began winning and was soon as right as rain."

Shelter staff named him Rademenes, after a cat from a Polish children's TV show, who is the reincarnation of a man who granted seven wishes to a boy who rescued him from thugs. And now, says Lucyna, "He cuddles and hugs other poorly animals. He cleans them, and sleeps with them, and pays particular attention to those suffering from serious disease. It's as if having been so close to death's door himself, he now wants to help others get better. We joke that he is now one of our full-time nurses."

. . . . . . . . . . . . . . . . . . . . . . . . . . . . .

## The lion who lives a life of compassion will receive it.

(Sumerian proverb)

Can I see another's woe,
And not be in sorrow too?
Can I see another's grief,
And not seek for kind relief?

**William Blake**
(From *Songs of Innocence and Experience*, 1866)

# Condition of the heart

In April 2016, the world said "goodnight, sweet Prince" to one of the greatest musicians of all time; a latter-day Mozart whose talent was so vast he would cheerfully give away songs that could revitalise or turbo-charge others' careers. With each passing year, it becomes ever-clearer that his godlike genius status is *under*estimated. Sometimes, as with the Beatles, artists sell millions of records because they are empirically and unequivocally outstanding. But this virtuoso was rather outstanding in other ways, too.

Fiercely private, little was known of Mr Nelson's philanthropic work until after his untimely death from a painkiller overdose. From his very first solo concert in 1979, a benefit for the Capri Theatre in New York City, and throughout his purple reign, the little guy with the big name quietly did his bit, without making a song and dance about it.

Political and environmental activist Van Jones is among those who had the inside track on His Royal Badness's benevolence. While working on the sustainability-oriented Green Jobs Act of 2007, Jones received an anonymous cheque for $50,000. He returned the cheque, only for it to be re-sent. As he related to Rolling Stone, Jones next received a call from a rock royalty representative: "I cannot tell you who the money is coming from, but his favourite colour is purple." The pair formed a friendship spanning many years and worked on several projects together, including Green for All, an advocacy group for green energy, and the Green Jobs Initiative, which gave jobs to young people of colour, installing solar panels. "There are people who have solar panels on their houses right now in Oakland, California, that don't know Prince paid for them," Jones told CNN.

Prompted by the fatal shooting of unarmed black teenager Trayvon Martin, the Artist was also instrumental in establishing #YesWeCode, an organisation that gives underprivileged girls and boys a head-start in the tech industry; a drive to create "black Mark Zuckerbergs", as Jones puts it. While in 2015, following the death of Freddie Gray in police custody, he held a Rally 4 Peace concert in Baltimore. "The system is broken... it's going to take the young people to fix it this time," he told the audience. The song Baltimore was written as a tribute to Gray, and other victims of police brutality – a tragic sign o' the times.

Stories of his secret gigs are legion. Often announced at the very last minute, and played in tiny venues, Prince appeared to really get off on giving back to fans. In 1984 he staged a free concert for deaf and blind students at Gallaudet College in Washington DC. While many gig-goers could neither hear nor see the specially toned-down performance, they all felt it. "God made you, God made me, he made us all equally," he sang that night, which no doubt struck a chord.

The truth is, we'll never know the full extent of his anonymous donations to countless organisations. "Just don't say anything about it" he'd tell his beneficiaries. He donated to everything from boxing clubs and libraries to the victims of a bridge collapse – and a local Minnesota school, Chanhassen Elementary, a few blocks from Paisley Park, to whose music department he gave $30,000: the biggest yearly donation it ever received. Teachers at the nearby Goddard pre-school won't forget the time he trundled in on his bicycle one day to say hi, either. Dig, if you will, *that* picture.

Yet, as another former Chanhassen local, Raisa Elhadi, says, "Financial support was only a fraction of what Prince gave us... his real gift to Chanhassen was a lesson: be colourful, be passionate, be glamorous, be unapologetic, and above all, be yourself." Among those of us gathered here today to get through this thing called life, Nothing Compares 2 certain individuals in particular.

• • • • • • • • • • • • • • • • • • • • • • • • • • • • •

Compassion is an action word with
no boundaries. It is never wasted.

**Prince**
(from an interview with Vegetarian Times, 1997)

Being the Queen is not all about singing, and being a diva is not all about singing. It has much to do with your service to people. And your social contributions to your community and your civic contributions as well.

**Aretha Franklin**
(From an interview with
Washingtonpost.com, 2008)

# Kindness tip

Be a part of your community, even in a small way. Attend local events. Volunteer if you can spare the time. Get to know your neighbours. And shop locally: it's estimated that for every £1 spent locally, between 50-70% circulates back into that community. Small, independent retailers are the lifeblood of the community, and they need our support now more than ever. Plus, keeping it local is better for the environment.

# The meaning of *ubuntu*

The Covid-19 lockdowns gave those of us accustomed to relative freedom a small insight into the lives of others. As days became weeks, we tried to be patient and find positive aspects to our changed circumstances, despite the deprivations and loneliness. But what if those days and weeks had become years and years?

What if we were imprisoned for 27 years?

In August 1962 the 44-year-old Nelson Mandela was arrested for his role in the African National Congress, the organisation fighting apartheid – the racial segregation of South Africa. Mandela was sentenced to five years' imprisonment, but the charges escalated to treason and, although he avoided the death penalty, he was condemned to life in prison.

The first years of Mandela's sentence at Robben Island Prison were served in a damp concrete cell, measuring just 8x7 ft, and with only a straw mat to sleep on. Verbally and physically harassed by white prison wardens, the prisoners were forced to break rocks into gravel and the glare from the stone permanently damaged Mandela's eyesight.

Permitted only one visit and one (heavily censored) letter every six months, Mandela's mother and his firstborn son both died within the first few years of his sentence, but he was forbidden to attend either funeral.

Mandela studied Afrikaans to help build a dialogue with the wardens and at night he worked on his law degree. Newspapers were forbidden and he served time in solitary confinement for receiving cuttings that had been smuggled into jail. Discovering several pages of Mandela's nascent autobiography, the prison authorities withdrew his study privileges for the next four years.

When he was finally released from prison in February 1990, the 71-year-old's walk to freedom was broadcast live across the world and, in 1994, Mandela was elected President of South Africa. Paying tribute to Mandela after his death in 2013, Archbishop Desmond Tutu wrote, "He set aside the bitterness of enduring 27 years in apartheid prisons – and the weight of centuries of colonial division, subjugation and repression – to personify the spirit and practice of *ubuntu*, or human kindness. He perfectly understood that people are dependent on other people in order for individuals and society to prosper."

Mandela used his position to publicly reconcile with his former captors, setting an example for the post-apartheid unification of the country. At his presidential inauguration ceremony, Mandela's VIP guest was a prison warder whose courtesy had set him apart from his colleagues. And Mandela adopted the sporting tradition of 'swapping shirts' when he wore the green jersey of the Springboks – once a symbol of oppression – to present the trophy to the South African captain at the World Cup final.

Mandela invited to lunch the state prosecutor who demanded that he receive the death penalty for treason, stating that the man was only doing his job. But it's the story of Christo Brand which perhaps best exemplifies Mandela's dignity and compassion. Brand was a pro-apartheid 18-year-old white prison guard when he first encountered Mandela, then 60. An unlikely friendship developed, based on mutual respect, with Brand breaking the rules to smuggle in not only bread and messages but also Mandela's favourite hair pomade. Incredibly, even his baby grandson was snuck in. Mandela wept as he cradled the infant for the first time. He encouraged the warder to continue his studies and gave him legal advice. Brand's experiences transformed his views about apartheid and years later he returned to the prison, now a museum, to manage its bookshop.

Mandela's dream for South Africa was to represent hope for the world: for every divided nation and warring neighbour. He embodied the spirit of forgiveness and reconciliation. He knew how to accept criticism and when to apologise. And above all, in times of freedom and lockdown, Nelson Mandela showed us how to live in peace.

Nelson Mandela, 18 July 1918 – 5 December 2013

# Unlocking their potential

One day in 2002, James Timpson visited his local prison and struck up a friendship with a 19-year-old prisoner called Matt. "I really liked his personality, so I offered him a job when he came out and he was great," says Timpson, the CEO of the high street dry cleaning, key cutting and shoe mending chain that bears his name.

And because of that encounter, some 1200 ex-offenders are now among its employees. Around 10% of the workforce are people with criminal convictions – people like former prisoner Sarah Barker, who was jailed after a violent assault and had been turned down by almost 70 companies before Timpson helped turn her life around. Around seven of the group's 2,000-plus stores are managed by people still serving their sentences, on day-release; Timpson has spent nearly £700,000 on their professional rehabilitation.

Timpson (whose logo is "Great Service by Great People") call their approach "upside down management", trusting their trainees to run the shops in the best way they see fit. "Prisons and re-offending cost the UK taxpayer approximately £11 billion per year," they say. "We believe that by offering people an alternative to crime, and enabling them to break the offending cycle, we can make a real difference in society." It's an initiative Frances Crook, chief executive of the Howard League for Penal Reform, has called "utterly wonderful".

That's not all. Timpson also clean the suits of unemployed people with upcoming job interviews totally free of charge. As James told BBC News in 2015, "When people are going for interview it's important to look and feel smart and getting their suit dry cleaned is part of that. It makes people more confident and gives them that 2% extra chance of getting a job. We just thought it was a really good idea."

And as for Matt? He went on to become one of their most successful branch managers.

# Goodness is the only investment that never fails.

**Henry David Thoreau**
(From *Walden*, 1854)

## Kindness tip

If you're in a position to invest,
think about where your money is going.
Do your research. What are the company's
sustainability goals? Do they look after
their workforce? Do they pay a living wage?
What does the company do in terms of
community outreach?

# Broom raiders

In August 2011, London was rocked by a series of riots, sparked by the fatal shooting by police of the unarmed Mark Duggan. The rioting spread to other cities such as Birmingham, Bristol, Manchester and Nottingham. Just as quickly, a social media-propelled clean-up operation sprang into action; if looters had used Blackberry Messenger to mobilize, the response would show Twitter at its best.

Accounts such as @Riotcleanup attracted scores of helpers, advising rubber-gloved and broom-wielding volunteers which areas needed clearing up. Elsewhere, a #riotwombles hashtag fired up, referencing the tidy little denizens of Wimbledon Common. Singers such as Kaiser Chiefs' Ricky Wilson and Kate Nash joined in the big clean. Nash raced around collecting donations for Tottenham Green Leisure Centre, so that affected locals (whose fingertips were holding onto the cracks in their foundations), could receive emergency supplies of clothes, food and baby products. "What really felt amazing yesterday was how many people were out in the streets, all day and night," Nash told reporters. "People literally sweeping the streets, taking the broken glass out of windows, gluing wood to broken doors and talking to strangers from all different types of class/race/gender and backgrounds. The atmosphere was positive and protective."

While hundreds of tradesmen offered to give up some of their time for free, high street banks gave financial support to businesses who'd lost stock, and Facebook's Operation Cup of Tea encouraged people to stay at home with a nice cuppa, donating the proceeds of tea bought through the platform to those who'd lost their homes. One feels Madame Cholet, Great Uncle Bulgaria and Tobermory would have heartily approved.

• • • • • • • • • • • • • • • • • • • • • • • • • • •

We are far more united than the things that divide us.

**Jo Cox MP**
(House of Commons speech, 19 June 2015)

# Alone we can do so little, together we can do so much.

### (Attributed to Helen Keller)

## Kindness tip

Bin day? Why not put your neighbours'
bins out at the same time as yours.
It's the worst chore in the world, and it's
only a few minutes out of your day.

# Penny sweets from Heaven

Is it a bird? Is it a plane? Well, yes, okay, it's a plane. But this plane has no ordinary pilot: it's Uncle Wiggly Wings to the rescue, with his rain of confectionery for the starving kids of West Berlin in the aftermath of World War II.

By 1948, with the Cold War heating up, Stalin was blocking rail, road and canal routes into the East German zone, choking the life out of its people. The newly created US air force soared into action, airdropping 13,000 tons of food, medicine and coal on the bombed-out city under codename Operation Vittles. Among the pilots was Gail Seymour 'Hal' Halvorsen, who'd been making daily drops from Rhein-Main Air Base in West Germany to Berlin's Tempelhof Air Field.

One day in July, while doing some amateur filming at Tempelhof, he bumped into some children lined up behind the perimeter fence. Initially, he was struck by their reluctance to ask for anything – so unlike the young'uns who chanted "Got any gum, chum?" at servicemen back home. As he'd relate in his autobiography, *The Berlin Candy Bomber*, "I reached into my pocket, but all I had were two sticks of gum. Right then, the smallest decision I made changed the rest of my life."

Breaking the Wrigley's Doublemint in half and passing it through the barbed wire, he promised to drop more sweets off when he was next flying over, if the kids (some of whom were ecstatically sniffing the wrappers) promised to share them around. But how would the children know which plane was his? Easy: he'd wiggle the wings of his C-54 Skymaster before dropping the goodies, attached to little hankie parachutes and fluttered down, 100 feet over their heads.

Tempelhof was soon inundated with letters, all addressed to the 'Chocolate Flyer' ('Der Schokoladen Flieger'). "You got me in a little trouble there, Halvorsen," Hal's squadron commander Colonel James R Haun told him, after pictures of the tiny parachutes began appearing in the newspaper. All the same, Haun agreed he could keep 'Operation Little Vittles' going, as long as he kept the top brass informed.

"It just went crazy after that," said Hal, as co-pilots donated their own sweets, officers' wives set to work sewing mini-chutes, and sweets and chocolates flooded in from the US which, just a few years previously, had been at war with Germany. As Hal later commented, "Person to person, people can get along. It's the system that's screwed up."

In all, he'd drop 23 tonnes of sweets – even sending them directly through the mail to one seven-year-old, so as not to frighten her pet chickens who mistook the C-54s for chicken hawks. In 1974, Germany awarded him its sole federal decoration, the *Großes Bundesverdienstkreuz*. But the man Berliner *kinder* knew only as 'Onkel Wackelflugel' hadn't yet hung up his wings.

In 1994, reports emerged that the Candy Bomber had struck again – in Bosnia. The retired pilot had persuaded the US air force to let him drop hundreds of chocolate bars 30 miles outside war-torn Sarajevo during relief effort Operation Provide Promise. "It was just like old times," he told press. "I'd just like to keep going over there and drop like mad."

At time of writing, the 100-year-old has just made a full recovery from coronavirus. *Sweet*.

• • • • • • • • • • • • • • • • • • • • • • • •

Human kindness has never weakened the stamina or softened the fibre of a free people. A nation does not have to be cruel to be tough.

**Franklin D Roosevelt**
(Radio address, 1940)

## Kindness tip

Let them eat cake! Take treats into the office – not because it's someone's birthday, but merely to give everyone a pick-me-up. And try to always have an emergency bar of chocolate on your person, for that tired and screaming toddler on the bus, or for someone feeling faint, or an inconsolable friend. You never know when it will come in handy.

This is my doctrine:
Give every other human
being every right you
claim for yourself.

**Robert G Ingersoll**
(From *The Liberty Of Man,
Woman And Child*, 1877)

# Kindness tip

While in conversation, think about what the other person is saying, as opposed to what you're going to say next. And when they really need somebody to talk to, and that person happens to be you, just listen, and allow them the vast majority of that conversation. In answering, don't make it about yourself. This is not about taking turns.

# The loveliness of the long-distance runner

2 December 2012, Burlada, Spain: through a rain of perspiration, Iván Fernández Anaya sees the retreating back of Abel Mutai, the Kenyan athlete who four months previously took bronze in the 3000-metre steeplechase at the 2012 London Olympics. Mutai is going to win this cross-country race. But then, as the two men enter the finishing straight, something unexpected happens. Misreading the signs on the track, the Kenyan pulls up some 10 metres before the finishing line. Keep going, the crowd shouts! But not being a Spanish speaker, Mutai doesn't understand. What happened next made headlines around the world.

As Fernández Anaya level-pegged, he realised what was happening and slowed down, and gestured to his rival to take the extra steps needed to win. As he later told press, "I didn't deserve to win it. I did what I had to do. He was the rightful winner. He created a gap that I couldn't have closed if he hadn't made a mistake. As soon as I saw he was stopping, I knew I wasn't going to pass him."

Added his coach, the former world Marathon champion Martín Fiz, "It was a very good gesture of honesty. A gesture of the kind that isn't made any more. I certainly would have taken advantage of it to win." Fernández Anaya himself plays it down: as he told Spanish newspaper El Pais, "In the Burlada cross-country race there was hardly anything at stake, apart from being able to say that you had beaten an Olympic medallist. But even if they had told me that winning would have earned me a place in the Spanish team for the European championships, I wouldn't have done it either."

. . . . . . . . . . . . . . . . . . . . . . . . . . . . .

## No act of kindness, however small, is ever wasted.

(Aesop)

It'll come home to
you all right, never fear.
Kind words is never lost,
nor acts neither.

**E Nesbit**
(From *The Wonderful Garden*, 1911)

## Kindness tip

No matter how competitive you are, try to be a
good sport. Whether you're competing in the
Olympics, or the three-legged race at your local
village fête, be gracious in defeat. Nobody likes a
sore loser. And conversely, be gracious in victory.

It is a little embarrassing
that after 45 years of
research and study,
the best advice I can give
people is to be a little
kinder to each other.

(Attributed to Aldous Huxley)

# Kindness tip

If you've committed to something, do it. Don't let people down unless you have a very good reason. We've all had those days when you're exhausted, and just want to curl up with a takeaway and watch Netflix. But consider the feelings of the person you are due to meet.

# Animal instinct

The tsunami of Boxing Day 2004 was one of the deadliest natural disasters in modern history. Triggered by a massive 9.1-magnitude earthquake in the Indian Ocean, it created waves of up to 500 mph and as much pent-up energy as thousands of atomic bombs. In just 10 minutes, countries including Thailand, Sri Lanka and Indonesia were devastated. It killed nearly 230,000 people and displaced tens of thousands of others.

Stories of kindness around these tragic events are legion. Alas, one legendary tsunami story is indeed just that: a legend. We can find no hard evidence that a group of elephants on the Thai island of Khao Lak rescued up to 50 tourists. The very thought of charging elephants scooping up bewildered tourists with their trunks and taking them inland to safety is highly improbable.

But consider the story of Ning Nong the elephant, who saved the life of eight-year-old British tourist Amber Owen. Amber was holidaying with her family on the island of Phuket and had struck up a great friendship with the four-year-old Ning Nong. Every day she'd ride him on the beach and feed him bananas, as he protectively wrapped his trunk around her. And that was their blissful routine on the morning of 26 December, too – up until the point the suddenly anxious pachyderm started edging away from the shoreline. And then a huge wave rushed the pair. Ning Nong fought the force of the water and charged towards higher ground with the young girl on his back, eventually depositing her to safety. The story later inspired the book *Running Wild* by former children's laureate Michael Morpurgo, and was adapted into a stage play.

"I want to go back to the beach," Amber told the Daily Mirror in 2016. "I'd like to see if he remembers me. Elephants have something special and a strong sense. They know what's going on before humans do. I thank him for my life."

Animals are sentient, intelligent, perceptive, funny and entertaining. We owe them a duty of care as we do to children.

**Michael Morpurgo**
(From a Guardian Q&A, 2011)

# The man with the golden autograph

Writer and comedian Marc Haynes was seven when he first met James Bond. He'd been waiting with his grandad at Nice Airport when he spotted the British superspy reading a newspaper near departures. Uttering the immortal words, "My grandson says you're famous – can you sign this?", Haynes senior approached the MI6 agent. And with immaculate charm, 007 duly inscribed his signature on the back of his boarding pass, "with all my love".

But instead of being thrilled, young Marc was crushed. Haynes senior marched back. "He says you've signed the wrong name. He says your name is James Bond." The man beckoned the boy over. Glancing from side to side and raising one famous eyebrow, he whispered, "I have to sign my name as 'Roger Moore' because otherwise... Blofeld might find out I was here." A delighted Marc headed back to his seat, shaken and stirred.

Many years later, Marc was working as a scriptwriter for a recording that involved UNICEF, for whom Moore was an ambassador. As the cameramen set up their equipment, Haynes reminded him of their previous encounter. "Well, I don't remember but I'm glad you got to meet James Bond," he chuckled. "And then," says Marc, "he did something so brilliant. After the filming, he walked past me in the corridor, heading out to his car, but as he got level, he paused, looked both ways, raised an eyebrow and in a hushed voice said, 'Of course I remember our meeting in Nice. But I didn't say anything in there, because those cameramen – any one of them could be working for Blofeld.'"

As Marc tweeted, "What a man. What a tremendous man." The story, posted the day after Moore died in May 2017, went viral on social media. But Haynes wasn't quite done: he'd share a photo of the autograph in question ("a key relic from my story") if he managed to raise £1000 for UNICEF. To date, he has raised nearly £3000. His word was his Bond.

# Live, and be happy, and make others so.

**Mary Shelley**
(From *Frankenstein*, 1818)

## Kindness tip

Never pass up a chance to pay a sincere compliment, or tell someone you're proud of them, be it a friend, a colleague or complete stranger. Just make sure it's appropriate, and that you mean it. And don't be creepy about it.

By doing the work to love ourselves more, I believe we will love each other better.

**Laverne Cox**
(From 'Hung Up on Our Bullies: Internalized Transphobia', www.huffingtonpost.com, 2011)

# Kindness tip

If you consider yourself an ally of the transgender community, consider using pronouns (he/him/she/her) on social media handles or email signature. This is a simple but effective way of showing your support.

# Radiating kindness

At 72, former plant engineer Yasuteru Yamada was enjoying a well-earned retirement after a life spent tinkering with big lumps of metal. Quietly settling down to watch telly one evening, he was greeted by scenes to make the blood run cold.

In March 2011, Japan was hit by the double whammy of a tsunami and a magnitude 9.0 earthquake. In the worst nuclear catastrophe since the 1986 Chernobyl disaster, a domino effect caused irreparable damage to the cooling systems of the Fukushima Daiichi Nuclear Power Plant. Reporters at the site later described scenes of carnage, twisted girders and crumpled trucks. And with its reactors in meltdown, the plant, as the BBC put it, was "spewing radiation". As Yamada watched hundreds of workers frantically attempting to repair the ruin, a thought occurred.

Fallout particles, or radioactive dust, can cause mutations, organ failure and even rapid death. To this day, crops growing near the deadly Chernobyl site are still riddled with radiation, well above recommended levels. So why subject young workers to an ordeal that could shorten their lives or leave them childless, when elderly plant specialists like him could take their place instead?

For Yamada, a cancer survivor, this wasn't so much heroism as common sense: "I am 72, and on average I probably have 13 to 15 years left to live," he told press. "Even if I were exposed to radiation, cancer could take 20 or 30 years or longer to develop… I will be dead before it gets me."

With the help of fellow engineer Nobuhiro Shiotani, Yamada found some office space, jumped on social media, and started assembling his 'Skilled Veterans Corps'. Very quickly he'd gathered hundreds of professional volunteers, all aged over 60 (and one 82-year-old), but also musicians, cooks and teachers – people like former primary school teacher Michio Ito, who at that point was volunteering in a café that gave work experience to those with learning difficulties. "I don't think I'm particularly special," Ito told the BBC. "Most Japanese have this feeling in their heart. The question is whether you step forward, or you stay behind and watch."

Initially, the Japanese government and the Tokyo Electric Power Company, who owned the plant, were what you might call politely sceptical. Some were less polite. Goshi Hosono, a Prime Ministerial aide, redubbed the Skilled Veterans Corps 'The Suicide Corps'. "We are not kamikaze," Yamada scoffed. "The kamikaze were something strange, no risk management there. They were going to die. But we are going to come back."

By this point, several exhausted young workers had stopped showing up, collapsed with heatstroke or were found to be practically glowing like beacons with illegal doses of radiation. And by July, having been lobbied by Yamada non-stop, the government finally accepted the offer of help. Doing their best to remain "humble" in the face of some presumably rather bruised corporate and political egos, the pensioners inspected the plant in person, made recommendations, pressed the plant for higher safety standards ("Because we don't expect a fee, we can speak to them as equals") and launched a programme to help rehouse those who'd been forced to flee the area. As the New York Times wrote, "Yamada has triggered a much wider debate about the role of the elderly in Japan and the meaning of volunteerism."

Today, the Skilled Veterans Corps is an established non-profit organisation, with some 700 active members and more than 1600 support members, undertaking educational and social initiatives. During an era when the elderly are often blamed for our current malaises, it is useful to be reminded of a time when they were prepared to sacrifice their lives for the coming generations.

• • • • • • • • • • • • • • • • • • • • • • • •

Be kind to your fellow-men; this is your first duty, kind to every age and station, kind to all that is not foreign to humanity. What wisdom can you find that is greater than kindness?

**Jean-Jacques Rousseau**
(From *Emile, or On Education*, 1762)

Compassion was the most important, perhaps the sole law of human existence.

**Fyodor Dostoevsky**
(from *The Idiot*, 1868)

# Kindness tip

Are you being kind to yourself? Whether you're suffering from Imposter Syndrome, setting yourself impossibly high goals or measuring yourself against others: stop beating yourself up.

Set aside regular time for some self-pampering, or do something you've always wanted to do. Being kind to yourself puts you in the best possible position to be kind to others. And treat yourself…
Buy the damn shoes.
(Buy the damn dress too!)

# It's good to talk

There's a well-known saying, often attributed to the Yoruba people of West Africa: "It takes a village to raise a child." The proverb refers, literally, to the fact that children from many rural African villages are raised by an extended family, and more generally – and perhaps more profoundly – that entire communities can positively contribute to a person's growth. No one is left out. Elsewhere, the Native American Talking Circle tradition allows everyone within the sacred circle to have their say, to talk through their problems and feel supported, to feel their voice has been truly heard.

In the West, where individuals are more atomised, social media often takes the place of a wider, ersatz family, and it can be tremendously supportive. But it also comes with risks: not everyone is compassionate, civil or necessarily has your best interests at heart. At time of writing, the coronavirus pandemic has forced most of us even further into isolation. Video conferencing is a poor substitute for the real thing, and the lack of human touch has been hard to bear, especially when just a simple hug releases the hormone oxytocin, which promotes wellbeing and relieves stress.

In Normal Times, two very different sorts of groups are doing valuable work in this area. The Death Cafe was formed around the ideas of Swiss anthropologist and sociologist Bernard Crettaz, who wanted to break the silence around 'the last taboo'. Inspired by Crettaz's 'Café Mortel' events, the late Jon Underwood, and his psychotherapist mother, Sue Barsky Reid, began running their own non-profit, pop-up model. The objective is "to increase awareness of death with a view to helping people make the most of their (finite) lives". Starter questions might include: "Cremation or burial?" or "Where would you like to be when you die?" This is a social franchise: anyone can use the name within "an accessible, respectful and confidential space", which could be a living room, or even a cemetery or a yurt, anywhere from London to Australia. There are some 12,000 already in existence across 74 countries, in which strangers meet, express themselves and come to terms with their own mortality. The common denominator is tea and cake – it makes potentially tricky conversations easier to digest.

Meanwhile, in an era in which the most common form of death for males under 50 is suicide, the Dublin Boys Club encourages men of all ages to drop their guard and honestly share their feelings with other guys. Founded in 2020 by meditation teacher Conor Creighton and Irish artist Maser, it describes itself as a space "where men can learn to communicate better with each other, and grow into the most authentic versions of themselves". The only rules: "No banter, no booze, keep it real and personal." And for many blokes, opening up without a drink (or several dozen) to hand is a supreme act of courage. As Maser told Extra.ie, "It's a beautiful thing to see big men being vulnerable and being exposed. That vulnerability is true strength – that takes a lot."

As with the Death Cafe, the Club, which meets monthly and has a WhatsApp group, has no fixed abode: it's popped up everywhere from prisons to storage containers, from LA to the Mojave Desert. Conversational topics can range from father-son relationships to what it means to be a man – anything to strip away layers of toxic masculinity like old wallpaper. Then they go hiking or swimming. "Sometimes the conversations can feel like we're wading through mud," Creighton told the Irish Times. "But the relief in knowing that you can talk to other men about your depression, your loneliness, your disenchantment with the life you've worked so hard to build for yourself, is worth the work."

• • • • • • • • • • • • • • • • • • • • • • • • •

Shall we make a new rule of life from tonight: always try to be a little kinder than is necessary?

**JM Barrie**
(From *The Little White Bird*, 1902)

# Giving without prejudice

Christmas Day 2016 was ruined for millions when it was announced that pop star George Michael had died of suspected heart failure, aged just 53.

In the year that saw the world turn on its axis both politically and culturally, with some of our greatest cultural icons snatched away far too soon, George's death was pretty much the final straw. But then something else happened. Among the outpouring of grief, stories began to emerge – at first in a trickle, then in a flood – of exactly what he'd been up to for all those years. George had been steadily and secretly carrying out acts of altruism that could melt a soul of ice.

While apparently alternating between a life of refreshingly candid recklessness and Lebowski-like stoner indulgence, George had evidently been watching a lot of daytime TV. In 2008, Lynette Gillard of Lancashire appeared on *Deal or No Deal*, hoping to win enough cash for her IVF treatment. Sadly, she didn't come away with the prize money. But the very next day, George was in touch with the TV production company and anonymously donated £9000 towards the treatment. By sheer coincidence, Lynette found out she was pregnant on the day George died, and gave birth to Seth Logan George Hart the following September – his middle-name a tribute to his benefactor (or father-figure, if you will).

Similarly, after Jo Maidment appeared on *This Morning* in 2010, talking about her fertility plight and the fact she'd been denied treatment on the NHS, George once again came to the rescue with a cheque for £15,000. "I got a phone call from a PA saying a businessman would like to donate some money for one cycle of IVF for you," Jo told This Morning. "I didn't believe it at first... and it took me a good few days to respond because that wasn't what I came on the show for, I wanted to help other people in my position. But then we agreed to it, because (the PA) said it was what this particular man wanted." Tragically, she suffered a miscarriage (George sent flowers). But after a second round of treatment, baby Betsy was born.

Meanwhile, the royalties from some of his most famous songs went to charity: the proceeds from 'Last Christmas' went to the Ethiopian famine relief; royalties from 'Don't Let the Sun Go Down On Me' were split between the London Lighthouse – an AIDS hospice, and Rainbow Trust – a charity supporting children with terminal illnesses, and their families. And monies from 'Jesus to a Child' went, appropriately, to Childline, for whom he was a patron. Additionally, he was a patron of umpteen other charities including Terrence Higgins Trust and Macmillan Cancer Support. He also privately donated £99,000 to an AIDS charity based in West Kenya, a game-changing amount of money for a small charity, ensuring they could continue their important work.

George was also known to give cash to complete strangers. In the days immediately following his death, stories surfaced about him tipping debt-ridden barmaids many thousands of pounds. Another report stated that he'd helped out anonymously at a homeless shelter, swearing fellow workers to secrecy.

George once chartered a flight to Lapland for hundreds of disabled children to meet Santa Claus, and showered them with gifts and toys. He played a free Christmas concert in London for NHS nurses, by way of thanks for taking care of his mother. And he bought John Lennon's 'Imagine' piano for £1.67 m and gave it to the Beatles Story museum, thus ensuring it stayed in John's hometown of Liverpool in perpetuity.

George Michael wrote the book on kindness. And he did so discreetly, unassumingly and with no hidden agenda.

• • • • • • • • • • • • • • • • • • • • • • • • • • • • •

I am the milkman of human kindness,
I will leave an extra pint.

**Billy Bragg**
(from 'The Milkman of Human Kindness', 1983)

# You can't take it with you

Charles 'Chuck' Feeney, billionaire co-founder of retail giant Duty Free Shoppers, wanted to die broke. After leading a life that would make a Trappist monk look like a Kardashian, he finally achieved his aim in 2020 at the youthful age of 89. For four decades Chuck anonymously chucked over $8 bn at charities, causes and colleges, including $3.7 bn for education, $870 m for human rights, $76 m for Obamacare campaigns and $270 m towards public healthcare in Vietnam. (Admittedly, he also set aside a teeny $2 m for his and his wife Helga's retirement, in their austere San Francisco apartment.) Commented Feeney on his philanthropy, "Try it. You'll like it!"

Elsewhere, MacKenzie Scott, the world's 18th-richest individual (worth $60.7 bn) and former wife of Amazon CEO Jeff Bezos, donated more than $4 bn in just four months during 2020, having signed the Giving Pledge, by which pledgees promise to give away the lion's share of their wealth. "This pandemic has been a wrecking ball in the lives of Americans already struggling," she wrote on the US blogging platform Medium. "Economic losses and health outcomes alike have been worse for women, for people of colour and for people living in poverty. Meanwhile, it has substantially increased the wealth of billionaires."

In all, Scott gave away some $6 bn during that year to charities, organisations, several black colleges and universities and food banks, in a move recorded as one of the biggest annual distributions ever made by a living person. "I have a disproportionate amount of money to share," she wrote. "My approach to philanthropy will continue to be thoughtful. It will take time and effort and care. But I won't wait. And I will keep at it until the safe is empty."

Meanwhile, Frances and Patrick Connolly celebrated their 2019 Euromillions lottery win by donating more than half of their £115 m to charity. The fifty-something couple, who were living in a rented terrace house in County Down, Ireland at the time of their win, weren't completely off their chumps: they did buy a five-bedroom bungalow in Hartlepool first. And flew to New Zealand to visit their daughter. But not first-class, as they thought the price was, frankly, extortionate.

"I'm never going to be part of the jet set," Frances, a Guardian reader, told press. Instead, the millionaire, who describes her own philanthropy as "a total joyride from start to finish", spends her days donating everything from laptops for carers to toiletries for refugees, and to soup kitchens for the homeless through two charitable trusts. "We sat down and kind of figured out what we thought would make a difference in people's lives," she said.

During the 2020 pandemic, the couple paid for PPE-making equipment, along with hot meals and vouchers for frontline workers. They've also given 1000 gifts to hospital-bound Covid patients who aren't allowed visitors. Frances, who suffers from Perthes' disease, which means she'll eventually have to use a wheelchair (hence the bungalow and not the castle one estate agent offered them), admits to splashing out on a pair of earrings, and plans to do a PhD in clinical psychology.

"Everybody asks 'how do you cope with that kind of money?'" she told the Belfast Telegraph. "Well, we didn't cope with that kind of money because we started getting rid of it within a week. I have no idea what it's like to be a 115-times millionaire because I never was – or, at least, I was for about 25 minutes."

## Kindness tip

Despite being the sixth richest country in the world, an estimated 8.4 million people are living in food poverty in the UK. There are over 2000 food banks in the UK, and most supermarkets have a donation point for a local food bank. Make it a part of your weekly shopping routine to add a couple of items. Do check what items are most in need that particular week, as it can vary wildly. We cannot live on a diet of baked beans alone.

# The angel of love

They call it the scorched-earth policy: the act of destroying everything and anything an enemy might find useful. And it's what Lord Kitchener did to the Boers during the ferocious Second Boer War of 1899-1902, which aimed to grind two independent Boer states into the dirt. Outnumbered 6:1, the ragtag guerrilla army of mostly Afrikaans farmers (Boer means 'Farmer') was no match for the 500,000-strong British Army. Under Kitchener's command, they destroyed crops, burned farmsteads and livestock, and poisoned the water supplies. Boer women and children were placed in tents – ostensibly for their own protection. The reality was somewhat different. Preceding the Holocaust by some 40 years, these were the first examples of something that would come to be known over the course of the new century by a more familiar term: Concentration Camps.

An outspoken critic of the British policy in South Africa, Emily Hobhouse almost single-handedly drew attention to the plight of the women and children in these camps – the first time an entire nation had been targeted for incarceration. Having heard reports they were dying (it's estimated nearly 30,000 perished in the camps, mostly children), she established the Distress Fund for South African Women and Children, setting sail from Southampton in December 1900 to see for herself.

Despite opposition, she gained entry to a camp in Bloemfontein and was shocked by the "scarcity of essential provision" and "wholly inadequate" accommodation. Visits to other camps revealed more of the same. The lack of soap was fobbed off with excuses that it was "an article of luxury". It's down to Hobhouse that soap was re-classified as a necessity, while she also worked to get kettles for clean water, and more food and straw mattresses.

In reports published by the Manchester Guardian, Hobhouse denounced the scorched-earth tactics, and the treatment of internees. It caused a national scandal and loss of public support for the war. While Kitchener dubbed her 'That Bloody Woman', this thorn in the government's side gained another horribly familiar sobriquet too: traitor. On a return visit to South Africa, she was manhandled, tied to a chair and eventually deported.

Undeterred, she continued to criticise the government and raise awareness. "No barbarity in South Africa was as severe as the bleak cruelty of an apathetic parliament," she wrote, forcing the government to investigate the dire situation. A commission headed by Millicent Fawcett confirmed pretty much everything Hobhouse had described – one in four Boer women and children had indeed died of disease, starvation and exposure in the overcrowded camps.

After the war she returned to South Africa, writing to the British press about the squalor the Boers were forced to live in, and set about distributing food, clothing and livestock feed. She created a network of schools for women and girls, teaching them practical skills such as spinning and weaving. In total, there were 26 such schools. She returned again in 1913 for the inauguration of the National Women's Monument in Bloemfontein, commemorating the women and children who died in the camps, and was made an honorary South African for her humanitarian work.

Despite ill health, Hobhouse undertook relief work in central Europe during World War I, then worked as a post-war representative for the Save the Children Fund, before health problems forced her to retire. Grateful South Africans raised enough money to buy her a house in her beloved Cornwall. She died, almost penniless, in June 1926, to little fanfare in the British press. That October, her ashes were carried to South Africa and interred at the base of the National Women's Monument. A fitting resting place for the socialist, anti-imperialist pacifist that Boer women called 'The Angel of Love'.

· · · · · · · · · · · · · · · · · · · · · · · · · · · · · ·

If you are not sure what you think about something, the most useful questions are these: are you being kind? Are they being kind? That usually gives you the answer.

**Jan Morris**
(From an interview in the Guardian, 2020)

# The folly and the ivy

Christmas Eve on the Western Front. As British troops huddled in their holes in the earth, an incongruous yet strangely familiar sound drifted out across the frozen wastes of No Man's Land. The Germans were carolling: 'Stille Nacht, Heilige Nacht'. Not only that, they were lighting lamps, erecting what appeared to be a Christmas tree – and calling for the enemy to come over and help them celebrate. As the Allies gawped in bleary amazement, a brave sergeant took his chances – and shortly returned with a handful of German cigars he'd exchanged for a can of Maconochie's stew. By now, the British had joined in the carolling. All pretty surreal. "But, as a curious episode," recorded Second Lieutenant Bruce Bairnsfather, "this was nothing in comparison to our experience on the following day."

Many people know, or think they know, the story of the famous Christmas Truce that took place in 1914. Some of this is myth-making. History is partial, in both senses. There was no mass-organised football match, for example. And only around half the Brits joined in: several unsporting chaps continued to pick off friendly, unarmed Germans, while sniping and shelling continued among several units who'd been unaware of it. But the positive actions that did occur were utterly spontaneous, heartfelt, and resonate to this day.

Back in Blighty, the holiday period carried on much as before; festive shoppers thronged the West End. Many people expected the Allies to have wrapped it up by Christmas. British casualties were relatively low. Reality had yet to hit hard. As Christmas approached, 101 British Suffragists signed an Open Letter to the Women of Germany and Austria, urging "our rulers to stay further bloodshed". Even the Pope suggested "the guns may fall silent at least upon the night the angels sang."

And for those in combat, the temporary armistice hadn't come completely out of the blue. During the first few months of the deeply unpopular Great War, there had been reluctance from soldiers to engage: an unspoken agreement arose that, unless they were actually shot at, they'd rather keep their heads down. Impersonal shells and mortar took the majority of lives, not bullets. Due to the proximity of their trenches, Germans and Allies going through the same experience, did share a certain grim camaraderie.

That Christmas morning, below the cloudless skies of northern France, weaponless Germans ambled through the mist towards the Allied trenches, holding up ceasefire signs written in English and shouting, "A merry Christmas, we don't fire!" Several had held jobs in England, and knew the language. (They were also winning at that point, which partly explains the largesse.)

"We shook hands, wished each other a Merry Christmas and were soon conversing as if we had known each other for years," British Corporal John Ferguson wrote of the encounter. "Here we were laughing and chatting to men whom only a few hours before we were trying to kill!"

The phenomenon spread in isolated pockets across the battlefield between individuals, who swapped cigarettes, buttons and food, and had little kickabouts among the craters. Where footballs weren't available, small sandbags and tin cans were substituted. No scores were kept, no games refereed. One fixture suggested by the 2nd Argyll and Sutherland Highlanders was abandoned because of shelling.

For thousands of servicemen, it was the first time they'd seen the enemy face to face, never mind strolled around and shook hands as if it were a sunny day beside the Serpentine rather than a limb-strewn field in Flanders. As Bairnsfather observed, "There was not an atom of hate on either side that day... it was just like the interval between the rounds in a friendly boxing match." For friend and foe, Christmas was a shared cultural experience, a legacy of Victoriana, with much the same trimmings, traditions and carols. The hiatus also gave them a chance to collect their dead.

At one point, a much-coveted German helmet was exchanged for some bully beef and plum and apple jam. "They asked for marmalade, but we had not seen any ourselves since we left England," one soldier reported. Beers were shared, and cries of "Hoch der Kaiser!" rang out, prompting cheeky rebuffs from the English.

In some units, the festivities went on for days. On New Year's Eve, the gregarious London Rifle Brigade finally waved goodbye to "a very drunken German" from their trench. Elsewhere, a Cameronian, who'd been left with the communal rum jar on Hogmanay, reeled blissfully across No Man's Land in front of Germans who cheered delightedly and held fire, as his comrades begged him to return, lest he face arrest. "Come oot and fetch us!" he cackled, taking an impudent swig.

The generals, who needed kills, were incandescent. This was a wilful act of disobedience, from both sides. Furious orders came, banning such fraternising. One particularly nationalistic young German huffed, "Such a thing should not happen in wartime. Have you no German sense of honour left?" It seems Corporal Hitler was roundly ignored.

And then the following year, it happened again – yet again, initiated by the Germans, but on a much smaller scale. By then, spirits had hardened like ice in the wake of poison gas, the torpedoing of the British ocean liner the Lusitania by a German U-Boat, and millions more dead. As one man told a war correspondent, "To Hell with Christmas charity and all that tosh. We've got to get on with the war."

But more than 100 years later, as various world leaders retreat under the shell of isolationism and self-interested ideologues and media moguls whip up hatred towards our neighbours, it is helpful to be reminded of a day when two nations came together to demonstrate a shared commitment to brotherhood, humanity and peace.

Love consists in this:
that two solitudes
meet, protect and
greet each other.

**Rainer Maria Rilke**
(From *Letters to a Young Poet*, 1904)

# Breakout hit

If *The Shawshank Redemption* were any more of a sleeper-hit, it would have been performed entirely by a cast of sloths. Nominated for seven Oscars, it limped away from the 67th Academy Awards without so much as a mini-hamburger. Fortunately, there is an afterlife: paroled by VHS (it wound up the most rented video of 1995), today this testament to the power of hope is the IMDb's top-ranked movie, routinely acclaimed as one of the greatest films ever made. It was also one of Nelson Mandela's favourite movies.

Bit of backstory, then: adapted from a Stephen King novella *Rita Hayworth and the Shawshank Redemption*, a movie version seemed a nailed-on-cert after the phenomenal success of 1986's *Stand By Me*. Enter writer Frank Darabont, who'd already made a short film from King's short story 'The Woman in the Room', and had a trio of horror screenplays under his belt, including a remake of *The Blob*. Despite *Screen International* referring to the latter's box office returns as "disastrous", Frank ached to be taken seriously as a director. With an adapted script in hand, he paid King $5000 for the rights to the prison break movie, refusing even to relinquish them for the cool $2.5 million offered by *Stand By Me*'s director Rob Reiner. Keen-eyed readers may discern a theme here to do with perseverance or something.

And then, a few years after its release, Frank received a little surprise in the post. It was the cheque he'd sent to King for the rights. King had stuck it in a little frame, and included a note: "In case you ever need bail money. Love, Steve."

King has form here: established in 1977, his 'Dollar Baby' agreement offers students or new filmmakers the rights to his short stories for just one dollar. Yes, sure, some of them aren't so great. But, y'know. It's there if needed.

One last thing: the dedication at the end of film, "In memory of Allen Greene", is a tribute by Darabont to his friend and first-ever agent, who died from AIDS complications just before *Shawshank* began shooting. Said

Frank, "I wanted to acknowledge not just his significance to my career but also that he was an incredibly decent, much-loved and much-missed person in the lives of those who knew him."

· · · · · · · · · · · · · · · · · · · · · · · · ·

In case you are watching this, and you ever wonder whether to write to anyone, always do. Because you'll be surprised how much of a difference it can make.

**Christopher Hitchens**
(Terminally ill, in an interview with Jeremy Paxman, *Newsnight*, 2010)

## Kindness tip

Send a postcard or a card to a friend.
Not because it's their birthday. Just because.
It doesn't have to be a grand gesture of
undying love, just a silly quote, a song lyric,
or a line from a poem. Just let them know
you're thinking of them.

# A gorilla of the community

In 2016, a gorilla named Harambe from Cincinnati Zoo was shot and killed by a zoo worker when a young boy climbed into his enclosure. It was a hugely controversial story, causing shockwaves across the globe; not only highlighting the potential danger of zoo animals, but also going a long way to raise awareness for better standards of care in zoos.

A lesser-known story from 20 years earlier had a very different outcome. On August 19 1996 an unidentified three-year-old boy evaded his mother for a few moments at the Brookfield Zoo in Illinois. The intrepid toddler somehow scaled a 20-foot wall and fell into the Gorilla Enclosure. Unconscious, and suffering from cuts and bruises, the young boy was approached by a female gorilla, one of seven in the enclosure.

Fearing the worst, spectators started to scream as eight-year-old Binti Jua made her way to the prone toddler. But Binti Jua (whose name means 'Daughter of Sunshine' in Swahili) confounded all expectations. She cradled the child, picked him up at the waist, and tenderly made her way to a safety hatch, where rescuers were ready and waiting. The boy spent four days in hospital, and made a full recovery (and no doubt dined out on the story for many years to come). Binti Jua became something of a celebrity, receiving hundreds of baskets of fruit from adoring fans.

Expert debates have raged as to whether Binti's actions were a result of her training at the zoo (she was raised by humans) or if this was an act of 'animal altruism'. We like to think it's the latter.

Gorillas are almost altruistic in nature. There's very little if any "me-itis". When I get back to civilization I'm always appalled by "me, me, me".

(Attributed to Dian Fossey)

## Kindness tip

When you're out and about in nature, remember you're imposing on another's natural habitat. Be respectful of any wild animals or birds you might encounter. Observe from a safe distance so as not to cause a fright. Don't make any sudden movements or loud noises. Don't feed wild animals, and don't leave any trace of your presence, such as litter.

# War and peace

Desmond Doss, who died in 2006, was a war hero. He was awarded the highest medals of honour, including the Purple Heart and, er, the Medal of Honor. He's had schools, training camps and stretches of American highway named after him, at least two statues erected to his memory, and was the subject of a Hollywood biopic, 2016's *Hacksaw Ridge*. All pretty straightforward. So here's the kicker: he was also a conscientious objector who, having signed up for combat, refused to carry a weapon or kill anybody.

Doss was a US army combat medic, serving in historic battles such as the Battle of Guam and the Battle of Okinawa. Despite being wounded four times (at one point he'd resembled a human pincushion), he'd go on to save the lives of 75 soldiers: while the military reckons the number of infantry he saved was closer to 100, Doss himself claimed a mere 50, so history records a compromise. Refusing to seek cover, he carried them, individually, to safety, under a hail of bullets and mortar fire. On another occasion he scrambled through a shower of grenades to rescue more. Doss's pacifism sprung from the fact that he was a devout Seventh-day Adventist (his repeated cry during battle was "Lord, please help me get one more"), but also born out of a determination never to touch a firearm after witnessing a fight between his dad and uncle when he was a kid.

All quite a turnaround for the softly spoken little guy who'd been bullied by fellow soldiers and superiors while in training, for everything from his vegetarianism to his refusal to train on Saturdays. His commanding officers even tried to have him discharged on grounds of mental instability. "I'd be a very poor Christian if I accepted a discharge implying that I was mentally off because of my religion," he told them at the hearing.

The irony in all this? Doss could have deferred his military service, but felt an ethical obligation to enlist.

# He showed me his scars, and in return, he let me pretend that I had none.

**Madeline Miller**
(From *Circe*, 2018)

## Kindness tip

If you can, give blood. Each donation helps save a life and there's no better way to say "Thank you for everything" to the NHS. The UK alone needs nearly 5000 people per day to give blood and around 135,000 new donors a year to replace those who can no longer give. It's quick to register and easy to do, with the actual donation only taking five to 10 minutes. You'll experience a real and lasting sense of achievement for your efforts, and they'll send you on your way with snacks.

You either believe
that people respond
to authority, or that they
respond to kindness and
inclusion. I think that people
respond better to reward
than punishment.

**Brian Eno**
(From an interview in Time Out, 2005)

# Kindness tip

As the old saying goes,
"If you haven't got anything nice to say, don't say anything at all." Never a truer word was spoken in these days of social media. By the same token, if you do love a certain TV show, film, book or whatever, TELL THE WHOLE WORLD ABOUT IT! A whole team of people have poured their hearts and souls into that project for months, or most likely years. They will love you for it.

# The power of glove

If the year 1968 could be reduced to a single image, it would be a great whirring dust cloud of fists, clubs and tank guns. This incendiary 12 months of uprisings, police brutality, political assassinations and unpopular foreign wars ended with an unscrupulous president being elected to the White House. (Seems like yesterday, don't it.) So 1968's controversial Summer Olympics in Mexico City was bang on trend, producing not just an unforgettable moment of sporting history, but one of the defining images of the civil rights movement.

It was 16 October, mere months after the murders of Martin Luther King Jr and civil rights ally Robert F Kennedy. Amid protests against the Vietnam War (in which Black Americans were more likely to be drafted than whites), African-American athletes Tommie Smith and John Carlos, along with a white Australian called Peter Norman, mounted the podium to display their medals for the 200 m final.

Like Carlos, Gold-medallist Smith, who'd set a world record in the process, wore no shoes. Instead he wore black socks, to represent black poverty, and a black scarf representing black pride. Carlos, awarded Bronze, had also unzipped his tracksuit top to show solidarity with blue-collar workers. Around his neck he wore a beaded necklace, "for those individuals that were lynched or killed and that no one said a prayer for, that were hung and tarred," he said later. All three wore Olympic Project for Human Rights (OPHR) badges. But only two were wearing one black glove each. And then the strains of the US National Anthem cranked up. And then all hell broke loose.

As 'Star-Spangled Banner' blared out, Smith and Carlos bowed their heads and raised their fists in a Black Power salute. It immediately caused shockwaves around the stadium and, thereafter, the world. Initially stunned into silence, the audience erupted in boos and racist insults as the pair were quickly ushered away, banned from the Olympic Village and suspended for turning the ceremony into a political statement. Time magazine wrote of the gesture: "'Faster, Higher, Stronger' is the motto of the Olympic Games. 'Angrier, nastier, uglier' better describes the scene in Mexico City last week." Death threats followed, though Smith and Carlos eventually went on to have successful careers in American Football.

But what of Silver-medallist, Peter Norman? While it may have appeared he was a passive onlooker, he'd actually been anything but. A devoutly religious man and a member of the Salvation Army, Norman believed all men were equal. Australia had its own racial tensions – the advent of the abhorrent 'White Australia Policy' sought to limit immigration for non-whites. Peter had taken a keen interest in the activities of the OPHR, and it was he who'd suggested all three men wore the badges on the podium. It was also Peter who'd suggested Smith and Carlos share a pair of black gloves and wear one each, after Carlos left his own pair behind at the Olympic Village.

The backlash was extraordinary. Despite qualifying for the 1972 Olympics and ranking fifth in the world, Norman was not sent to the Games in West Germany, and never competed in the Olympics again. He retired from the sport and suffered bouts of depression, alcoholism and painkiller addiction. He was not invited to the Opening Ceremony of the 2000 Sydney Olympics, though the Australian Olympic Committee denied that it excluded him.

He remained friends with Smith and Carlos, who were pallbearers at his funeral in 2006, and gave eulogies. They were also instrumental in creating 'Peter Norman Day' in recognition of his actions. In 2012, the Australian government issued a formal apology for "failure to fully recognise his inspirational role before his untimely death" and he was posthumously awarded the Order of Merit.

Despite it costing him his career, and his happiness, Norman never regretted his actions. He told the New York Times in 2000, "I ended up running the fastest race of my life to become part of something that transcended the Games." And that truly is the Olympic Spirit.

# A proper send-off

In July 2017, a body washed up in a cove at Cuckmere Haven, in East Sussex, England. The injuries suggested a woman had fallen – or been pushed – from a great height. After a year, despite a global police hunt and artists' impression of a (possibly trafficked) European aged between 25-55 with a distinctive silver necklace, nobody had come forward to claim her.

Enter Christina Martin, who in a previous life was a well-regarded stand-up comedian and prolific letter writer to Viz comic, and who currently works for Rother and Wealden District Councils where she is responsible for public health and welfare funerals. Part of Christina's remit (in a post actually invented for her) is attempting to track down friends and families of the deceased, who are often penniless individuals without next of kin or surviving relatives.

It's proper detective work. In instances where there's a name, she's able to track down a friend or two, or get a neighbour along to the funeral – usually depressingly unattended, save for a presiding council official. Occasionally, it turns up some random loveliness: an award-winning gardener; a carpenter and electrician who designed and filled his home with his own model railway; or a man who maintained to his bemused carers that he'd bought his business with buried treasure (and as his estranged family confirmed, was a detectorist who'd sold a valuable coin he'd unearthed).

And then the case of the Unknown Woman landed across Christina's desk. In a last-ditch bid to identify her through social media, newspaper reports, homeless charities and trafficking organisations, Christina inadvertently sparked something rather amazing in the local community. Despite burying her with no name, the Unknown Woman had a higher turnout than Christina could have possibly expected.

On 25 September 2018, in brilliant sunshine, a procession of 115 people followed the coffin's journey to its graveside at Hailsham Cemetery and laid a mountain of flowers, many donated by local florists after an appeal. There were readings, poems, a recitation of the Lord's Prayer, a chorus of Leonard Cohen's 'Hallelujah' – and a wake in a local pub, funded by well-wishers Sarah Taylor and Maria Lozano. A book of condolences was also placed there, in case her relatives ever did show up.

So remarkable was the turnout it made the local BBC evening news. As a Hailsham councillor observed, "Nothing like this ever happens to our sleepy, near-forgotten town." Hailsham doesn't even have a railway station. No one could recall another occasion when a pair of security men had been required at the cemetery gates, albeit they were barely needed: the media scrum was as limited as it was unobtrusive. "I think this speaks to all our fears about being alone at the end, or forgotten," Christina told reporters. "I guess because she's nobody's, she's all of ours. We all feel responsible for her."

In April 2019, a headstone was finally laid at the grave of the individual still known as the Unknown Woman, donated by a Sussex-based stonemason. These days, Maria tends the grave and has built a fence around it, planted a rose bush and placed an angel statue there. "I've had the rare privilege of rounding off someone's life," says Christina, "a life that might otherwise go unremarked upon. If a job's worth doing, especially if it's a job to do with people's lives, it's worth doing properly. Nowadays I'm back to more conventional cases, though none are normal, every life is different. I've yet to put on an unattended funeral, and I hope to keep it that way."

The moon shone fiercely on the night of the Unknown Woman's funeral. After an incredibly emotional day, Christina drove to Bexhill Beach to gaze at its almost supernatural beam, lighting up the sky like a gigantic alien mothership, and sprinkling its light over the pebbles in handfuls of silver. As Christina watched, it appeared to shine directly on Beachy Head, high above the spot where the Unknown Woman was originally found.

# The greatest tackle of all

Growing up in Wythenshawe, South Manchester, young Marcus Rashford relied on a spirit of community: the family friends and neighbours who'd drive him to football practice when his single mum was at work, or the teacher who'd drop him off at the end of his street. The kind of teamwork, public-spiritedness and care the future England striker would come to consider a fundamental spur to real change.

As he'd write years later, "Without the kindness and generosity of the community I had around me, there wouldn't be the Marcus Rashford you see today: a 22-year-old black man lucky enough to make a career playing a game I love." During the raging skip fire that was 2020, he'd end up directly influencing social policy – and force the government into making two U-turns over child food poverty to boot.

Rashford had already made headlines after visiting children who'd been wounded in the 2017 Manchester Arena terrorist attack, and by speaking out against systemic racism in football. In October 2019 he joined forces with the retailer Selfridges to personally deliver essential items to the homeless over Christmas. As he told ESPN.com, "It's a no-brainer for me, I think. Why not? For me, this type of stuff is making a bigger difference to our lives than just giving them money."

But his road to activism properly began in March 2020, during the first pandemic lockdown, after schools shut their gates. While recuperating with a back injury from an FA Cup replay against Wolverhampton, the Man-U number 10 teamed up with charity FareShare to send free meals to vulnerable children who normally received them during term time. As he tweeted, "I've spent the last few days talking to organisations to understand how this deficit is going to be filled... No child should have to worry where their next meal is coming from."

It wasn't just schools, as the England striker pointed out: community centres and breakfast clubs typically provided "the only meal many kids get each day". The initiative went national, the charity raised £20 m – and Rashford's undisclosed sum was the single largest donation.

In April, he joined the Players Together initiative, supporting NHS staff, before writing an open letter to MPs in June, calling for an end to another pandemic: UK child poverty. "Can we not all agree that no child should be going to bed hungry?" It worked: the next day, the government agreed to an extension of free school meals during the summer holidays. His Child Poverty Task Force followed in September; his MBE the month after.

Businesses and councils picked up the baton: the Co-operative Group provided 1000 food vouchers for kids during the October half-term, and a nationwide drive followed. In November, the government caved in yet again, pledging free meals to disadvantaged children over Christmas; a £400 m funding package for cash-strapped families to feed themselves that coming winter.

That same month Rashford launched a literacy campaign, a book club with Macmillan Children's Books to help underprivileged kids discover the joy of reading. "There were times where the escapism of reading could have really helped me," said Rashford, who "only started reading at 17, and it completely changed my outlook and mentality. I want this escapism for all children. Not just those that can afford it."

Towards the end of an extraordinary year, he turned his attention to the issue of social security, calling for a permanent £20 increase in universal credit. One of the grimmest ironies of lockdown is that families who were more comfortably off would likely emerge with increased savings, due to a lack of commuting or eating out. Conversely, research from the Resolution Foundation discovered that low-income families, who'd often been creatively adept at managing on limited budgets, were finding these same strategies "difficult if not impossible, to sustain". School closures were also eating into the budgets of struggling families, in the shape of extra food and energy bills – not to mention the costs incurred for remote learning: laptops and broadband connections don't grow on trees. If emergency credit top-ups were abandoned by the spring, hundreds of thousands of children would be driven into poverty. "I'm really concerned that families are constantly counting down the days until help is taken away from them," he tweeted. "The need for long-term change is massive. Children cannot be living to deadlines."

And then, in January 2021, photos emerged of what some of those free school meal parcels looked like: half a pepper, a potato, a carrot stub and some scraps of tuna in a coin bag. The sight of these pathetically inadequate five-day packages, issued in place of a £30 voucher, would have been laughable, were it not all so utterly tragic. A furious Rashford blasted the images as unacceptable. "If families are entitled to £30 worth of food, why is their delivery only equating to just over £5? Children deserve better than this." He has since called on the government to lower the age of free school meal eligibility, effectively aiding a further 1.7 million children coming from families on universal credit, while continuing to campaign to end child food poverty in Britain for good.

Here's the crucial point: Rashford isn't just plugging gaps and doling out Band-Aids willy-nilly, and he's certainly not just paying drive-by lip-service to the issues of the day. The man is effecting real social mobility, the kind that genuinely changes lives. In the space of a single year, amid tabloid and Tory sniping and racist abuse on social media, this smart, passionate, articulate (not to mention quite brilliant) footballer has arguably achieved more than most MPs have managed in a decade. At time of writing, he's still at it, hitting the phones, talking to charities and food industry bosses. If you're reading this book in the future, he's probably Prime Minister. Like a benign Terminator, Marcus Rashford Just. Keeps. Going.

Together we have demonstrated the power of kindness and compassion. We have shown that when it comes down to the wire, we will always have each other.

**Marcus Rashford**
(Twitter post, November 2020)

# Useful Organisations

If this book has inspired you to get involved, here are just a few of our favourite organisations which are doing wonderful things.

**Battersea Dogs & Cats Home**
Established in 1860, Battersea is there for every dog and cat, helping over 7000 animals every year.
www.battersea.org.uk

**Beauty Banks**
Beauty Banks supplies personal care and hygiene essentials to people in the UK who can't afford them. Because everybody has the right to be clean.
www.beautybanks.org.uk

**BYkids**
BYkids provides children around the world with the training and equipment to make documentary films tackling subjects such as immigration, bullying, climate change and social justice. They create understanding with storytelling.
bykids.org

**Campaign Against Living Miserably (CALM)**
Every week in the UK, 125 people take their own lives. Three-quarters of them are male. CALM campaigns to spread awareness of the devastating impact of suicide. It also provides frontline services for anyone at crisis point, and those bereaved by suicide.
www.thecalmzone.net

**Combat Stress**
Combat Stress provides specialist support for former servicemen and women, and their families. It helps people dealing with issues such as PTSD, anxiety and depression.
combatstress.org.uk

**Computer Aid**
Helping to bridge the digital divide, Computer Aid receives donations of computers, phones and tablets which are data-wiped, refurbished and distributed all over the world to those that need them.
www.computeraid.org

**Death Cafe**
People gather to drink tea, eat cake and discuss death. A discussion group, rather than a grief support session, Death Cafe aims to increase awareness of death with a view to helping people make the most of their lives.
deathcafe.com

**Dementia Friends**
Dementia Friends is an initiative from the Alzheimer's Society, aiming to change people's perceptions of dementia – i.e. how people think and talk about the condition.
www.dementiafriends.org.uk

**Dolly Parton's Imagination Library**
This is a book-gifting programme devoted to inspiring a lifelong love of reading. From birth until school age, children receive free books, regardless of their family's income.
imaginationlibrary.com

**Dublin Boys Club**
This organisation has clubs based all over the world, exploring healthy masculinity. Men learn to communicate better and become the most authentic versions of themselves.
www.thedublinboysclub.com

**Elton John AIDS Foundation**
The foundation funds frontline organisations around the world to prevent infection, challenge stigma and provide care for the most vulnerable groups affected by HIV.
www.eltonjohnaidsfoundation.org

**FareShare**
A network fighting food poverty in the UK and tackling food waste. They save good food from going to waste and redistribute it to frontline charities.
fareshare.org.uk

**Give blood**
Give blood tells you everything you need to know about how to donate and why this is so important.
www.blood.co.uk

**Habitat for Humanity**
A global non-profit housing organisation, working in over 70 countries, Habitat's vision is a world where everyone has a decent place to live. It helps people to build their own homes alongside volunteers, and to pay an affordable mortgage.
www.habitat.org

**Holocaust Educational Trust**
The Trust works in schools, universities and the community to raise awareness and understanding of the Holocaust. They provide teacher training, teaching aids and resource material.
www.het.org.uk

**Homeless Stories**
This is a project featuring first-person video accounts of people affected by homelessness. It's part of Stories for Change, a global storytelling platform aiming to highlight social issues.
homelessstories.co.uk
storiesforchange.org.uk

**Honeypot**
Honeypot provides help, advice and respite breaks for young carers with responsibilities beyond their years, giving them the chance to be a child again.
www.honeypot.org.uk

**HOPE not hate**
HOPE not hate uses education, research and public engagement to combat racism and help build communities that are inclusive. It does so by listening, organising, engaging and educating.
www.hopenothate.org.uk

**Limbs International**
Transforming lives, one step at a time, by providing high quality, low-cost prosthetic limbs for amputees in the developing world, who have limited access to medical care and prosthetics.
www.limbsinternational.org

**Magic Breakfast**
Providing healthy school breakfasts to children living in food poverty in the UK.
www.magicbreakfast.com

**Phone Credit for Refugees**
Helps refugees and displaced people all over the world, providing mobile phone top-ups so they can stay in touch with their families, communicate with support agencies and stay safe.
www.pc4r.org

**Reprieve**
Reprieve is a Legal Action non-governmental organisation (NGO) comprising lawyers, investigators and campaigners. They defend marginalised people facing human rights abuses and put the spotlight on cases of injustice.
reprieve.org

**Sightsavers**
This organisation works to eliminate avoidable blindness, promote equality for people with disabilities and advocate for change.
sightsavers.org

**Stemettes**
Stemettes helps the next generation of females and non-binary people access careers in STEM (Science, Technology, Engineering and Mathematics) by way of programmes, events and content for ages 5-25.
Stemettes.org

**Stonewall**
Stonewall campaigns for the equality of gay, lesbian, bi and trans people across the UK. It also provides information and support for LGBTQ+ communities, and their allies.
www.stonewall.org.uk

**Suspended Coffees**
A worldwide movement, a suspended coffee is the advance purchase of a cup of coffee (other beverages are available) for anyone that needs it. No questions asked. No matter why.
suspendedcoffees.com

**The Water Project**
This organisation provides access to reliable, safe, clean water across sub-Saharan Africa, one community at a time.
thewaterproject.org

**Thrive**
The gardening for health charity, Thrive works with people with disabilities or ill health, the disadvantaged and the vulnerable. They use an approach called Social and Therapeutic Horticulture (STH) to help improve physical and mental health.
thrive.org.uk

**Womankind Worldwide**
This organisation works with women's rights organisations and movements all over the world to create a better future for women and girls. They work towards ending all forms of violence, advancing women's economic rights, and strengthening women's influence.
www.womankind.org.uk

**Working Chance**
Working Chance is the UK's only charity supporting women leaving the criminal justice system into great jobs. Working with employers across all sectors, finding jobs with real career prospects for women who might otherwise struggle and have a high chance of reoffending.
workingchance.org

# INDEX

# KINDNESS IS POWER

Marcus Rashford

## Acknowledgements

Special thanks to Stephanie Milton, Lord Michael Cashman, Philippa Perry, Billy Bragg, Alexandra Pringle and Sarah Burns. And enormous thanks to Tony Lyons for our beautiful cover. The authors would also like to thank: Anastasia, Katherine Armstrong, Alice Jones Bartoli, David Bennun, Hanna Berrigan, Nicola Blackman, Jearl Boatswain, Mair Bosworth, Lynn Bowles, Karen Box, Emma Bradshaw, Juliet Brando, Vivienne Elisabeth Breton, Kate Brown, Anthea Bull, Ari Burleigh, Fraser and Kate Burns, Sheila Burns, Clare and Ghost Buxton, Annemarie Cancienne, Topsy Cat, Peter Chilvers, Roger Clarke, Richard Clark-Monks, Deborah Cleland-Harris, Mandy Colleran, Phoenix Curland, Lysanne Currie, The Davids, Dan Davies, Kate Dewey, Laila Dickson, Elise Dillsworth, Alex Donohoe, John Doran, Brian Eno, Flic Louise Everett, Stuart Finglass, Jane Fluckiger, Caroline Frost, Terry Gaussiat, Nadene Ghouri, Stella Giatrakou, Sara Gibbs, Matt Glasby, Anna Goodman, Kirsten Grant, John Green, Kate Griffiths, Luke Haines, Hazel and Ibrahim Hamad, Stacey Hamilton, Gill, Moayad, Nadia and Sara Hanoush, Maddie Hanson, Robyn Haque, Sophie Harris, Andrew Harrison, Phil Harrison, Jennie Harwood, Behiye Hassan, Marc Haynes, Jason Hazeley, Simon Hess, Ellen Holgate, Molly Holt, Jane Hudson, Simon Hughes, Jo Humphreys-Davies, Graeme Hunter, Joss Hutton, Sharon Hutton, Linda Innes, Penelope Ironstone, Marie Irshad-Nordgren, Kevin Jackson, Jeff Jamieson, Cath Janes, Sasha Jenkin, Holly Johnson, Davey Jones, Haydn Jones, Tejinder Jouhal, Vincent Kelleher, Saoirse Keogh-Moore, Emma Kidd, Suzanne King, Eartha Kitten, Rachel Knightley, Zosia Knopp, Blair Kutrow, Robin Lee, Georgia Lewis, Ruth Logan, Richard Luck, Helen Lusher, Penny Lyons, John Lyttle, Serena Mackesy, Jessica Mair, Perminder Mann, Izzy Mant, Christina Martin, Mhairi McFarlane, Fran and Steve McNicoll, Franny McSweeney, Maggie McSweeney, Vicki Mellor, David Miaowie, Suzanne Moore, Alex Morris, Joel Morris, Kieron Moyles, Stephen Neale, Kate Newport, Geri O'Donohoe, Fiona O'Hare, Victor Olliver, Kate Parkin, Annie Pepers, Amanda Percival, Keiron Pim, Tim Pollard, Paul Putner, Emma Quick, Justin Quirk, Julia Raeside, Kate Ray, Raoul and Carlyle Reedy, Ffyon Reilly, Oliver Reynolds Gili, Sian Rider, Vic Roberts, Kevin Sargent, Habie Schwarz, Alan Scollan, Nick Scott, Annie Shaw, Ben Shaw, Rick Shaw, David Smith, Nikki Smith, Paul Smith, James Snodgrass, Jon Spira, Nick Stearn, David Stubbs, Fiona Sturges, John Sturgis, Rose Taït, Isobel Taylor, Siobhan Tighe, Andrea Tome, Michelle Tuft-Smith, Law Turley, Matt Turpin, Maggie Walsh, Duncan Watson, Sarah Watts, Jessica Webb, Dominic Wells, Helen Wicks, Mark Williams, Nia Williams, Jonathan Wright, Elaine and Mary Wycherley, Steve Yates. And huge thanks to everyone at Bonnier.

159